April 15, 23

Best of greetings
Dr: Soju/Susan

author,

അഭിഷേക്കിലെ ങ്ങളുടെ
ലാസ്

Calgary
April 15, 2023

Best of greetings
Dr: Sola/Suson

author.

Think!

anindocanadian

ARCHWAY
PUBLISHING

Archway Publishing books may be ordered through booksellers or by contacting:

Archway Publishing
1663 Liberty Drive
Bloomington, IN 47403
www.archwaypublishing.com
844-669-3957

Because of the dynamic nature of the Internet, any web addresses or links contained in this book may have changed since publication and may no longer be valid. The views expressed in this work are solely those of the author and do not necessarily reflect the views of the publisher, and the publisher hereby disclaims any responsibility for them.

Any people depicted in stock imagery provided by Getty Images are models, and such images are being used for illustrative purposes only. Certain stock imagery © Getty Images.

Scripture quotations are from] The Catholic Edition of the Revised Standard Version of the Bible, copyright © 1965, 1966 National Council of the Churches of Christ in the United States of America. Used by permission. All rights reserved worldwide.

ISBN: 978-1-6657-1936-0 (sc)
ISBN: 978-1-6657-1935-3 (e)

Library of Congress Control Number: 2022903394

Print information available on the last page.

Archway Publishing rev. date: 02/24/2022

Dedicated to those who are afflicted with leprosy.

There is no certainty about anything. Good times and bad times come and go. Man is searching for something. Nobody knows the secret of the Universe.
—Kumaaran Ashaan

CONTENTS

Calgary

2022 AD

Dear Readers,

"Think!" contains thoughts from 1975, 1980, and 2016. I thought about tying them together, or scrapping them and starting from scratch. It would take a lot of scratching. Even then, there are bound to be ideas and thoughts that are rambled and often repeated. To avoid such a situation, at the end of the book, I have added a segment: "Fragmented, Remnant Thoughts." You may want to read this segment first, because I consider these as super thoughts, somewhat radical and revolutionary, but at the same time lighter. Let me say that I am here to provoke thoughts!

Cordially Yours,

ആന്റമ്പിറോട്ടേറ്റിയൻ

anindocanadian

INTRODUCTION

If the earth was flat, and if one was to look down on it from a high-flying satellite, through a powerful telescope, one could visualize the earth to be a gigantic movie studio, set up with scenes of mountains, plains, deserts, and oceans, all with great many artistic details that change their shades with the changing seasons. The light directors on this giant stage would be the sun, the moon, and the stars. The sound directors would be the wind, the waters, and the birds.

I think of life as an extravaganza, a giant stage production in which living organisms act. Each species may act out a particular role, but each actor, even in the same species, is a unique character.

The most important drama on earth may be that of man. Unlike other species, Homo Sapiens are known to modify the natural scenes, and even write the script for their own life dramas. For that matter, man even writes the script for other species. We reset the scenes on earth, by erecting big cities and moving machines. With electric lamps, we alter the lighting on the stage. The roar of our machinery produces unique sound effects. The story of the human drama is unfinished. It is a series of scenes with changing themes. The script is always written for the continuation of the present scene or in preparation for the scene coming after. Some scenes are comedies, and some are tragedies.

Any play written about man and produced on stage is a depiction of real life. Characters on stage represent characters in real life. Drama on the stage is taken from real life. Actors emulate characters, who have lived or known. However, an actor on stage is more aware of his acting and is less serious, because it is someone else's story that he is reenacting. The concept of life being a giant stage production is, I believe, a meaningful way to perceive living.

1

THE ROLES THAT PEOPLE PLAY

What Moves the Actor?

Acting is a stimulus response. A stimulus can be a desire or a thought, or it can be the way one is treated. The stimulus can come from various sources, and one's response to them is formulated into acting.

First, let us look into acting, as a response to a desire. I prefer to use the term desire over the term need, because a need is a term denoting survival (apt in describing animal urges), whereas desire is a more descriptive term for human aspirations. Desire can be physical, psychological, social, or spiritual. Then such distinctions only serve, as convenient means for conceptualizing. Think of a man who works to satisfy his physical desire to eat. In the process, he could be taking care of his psychological desire to be independent, his social desire to interact, and his spiritual desire to share the bread with the rest of his family. In fact, it is difficult to draw lines among these desires.

Each man acts according to the desires that are typical of him, and each makes use of talents that are inborn and acquired. The priorities of a confirmed bachelor may not be the same as those of an established family man. In any event, most desires are typical of every man. Some of the human desires are for food, security, recreation, health, appearance, sex, creativity, honor, prestige, power, fame, glory, and so on. Desire makes one act toward its fulfillment.

A quick word about desire. Desire can be viewed as being caused by (1) the genetic and biochemical makeup of human beings, (2) the sensorium (i.e., the physical apparatus for seeing, hearing, touching, smelling, and tasting and their counterparts in the brain), and (3) the different internal and external organs and the systems, (4) the faculty of intelligence (i.e., all the mechanisms involved in learning), and (5) the faculty of consciousness (i.e., the mechanisms involved in awareness of environment, self, and others in relation to one another). Then again, they can be simplified as physical, mental and spiritual faculties. A detailed explanation of this will follow later.

The workings of the above faculties cause desire. In turn, desire causes a state of unrest or tension. Tension can be positive or negative. A negative tension often follows a desire that is beyond one's personal capabilities. Such a desire seems unattainable, and the tension is negative. Similarly, a desire backed by one's personal resources produces positive tension, as the person realizes that he or she could materialize a wish, by making use of talents in positive acting. Negative tension can also result in positive acting for one who looks upon it as a challenge. Positive tension could result in negative acting for a villainous character. There are many stages that relieve one from tension. One way is by immediate emotional acting, resulting in an immediate and partial release of tension, but that does not necessarily fulfill the desire. This could constitute a facial, physical, or verbal expression. Following positive tension, people smile, dance around, shout for joy, announce a future plan, and act sensuous, romantic, shy, aggressive, or outspoken. Negative tension makes people cry out, swear, bite their teeth, strike out or act sad, anxious, fearful, or nervous. The relief is temporary, and the tension persists.

To get rid of the persistent tension and fulfil the desire, one seeks out concrete acting. Concrete acting could be work, play, or leisure. It may result in the fulfillment of the desire, or it may fail to fulfill the desire. With both success and failure, immediate emotional acting follows. It consists of a facial, physical, or verbal expression. This may again be followed by concrete acting—to either laugh with the joy of success or mourn the despair of failure. It could be a drinking bout in both cases.

A chain of desire, tension, emotional acting, concrete acting, could be established on a long-term basis, in certain instances. Persistent failure may cause repression of the tension. Inability to execute one's desires also causes repression of the tension. Long-term repression may result in maladjustment or even abnormal behavior. In both cases, acting becomes acting out.

Here is a hypothetical equation of acting: Desire → Tension → Emotional acting with partial and temporary relief of tension → Further tension → Concrete acting → Success or failure →

Emotional expressions of success or failure → Concrete acting that is followed (in some cases).

For example: Desire for food → Hunger → Emotional expressions of hunger (e.g., a sad facial expression, or whining, or stating that one is hungry) → Temporary and partial relief → Persistent hunger → Eating → Relief → Emotional expressions of relief (e.g., a smile or saying how good the food was).

Acting could take another channel, if food is unavailable. For example: Desire for food → Hunger → Emotional expressions of hunger → Temporary and partial relief → Further tension → Do not eat → No relief → Emotional expressions of no relief → Looking for food, begging for food, stealing food, or even striking out.

As was mentioned earlier, desire is not the only stimulus that causes acting. Certain presented situations will also cause one to act. For example: Get slapped → Anger → Emotional expressions of anger (like gnashing of teeth, banging the table, or hyperventilating) → Partial and temporary relief → Still angry → Slap the slapper → Relief → Emotional expressions of relief (like laughing). Or: Get slapped → Anger → Emotional expressions of anger (like blinking the eye or shaking the head) → Unextinguished anger → Reason out and act constructively → Relief.

The above is an example of a negative tension bringing about positive action. If one cannot get rid of anger, through either of the above ways, one may resort to crying, cursing, or shouting. If all of the above do not occur, repression may result. Repeated repression could decrease one's ability to tolerate frustrations—or in other words, increase one's temper.

Seeing or hearing can also trigger acting. For example, while watching television, one could be inspired: Watch a program on TV about the destitute in the developing world → Compassion → Emotional expression of compassion (like tears or grimace) → Temporary and partial consolation → Offer an affordable assistance → Relief → Announcement to relatives as expression of contentment. If situations like these bring tension without a release through concrete action for a lack of psychological resources, repression occurs and oversensitivity develops.

The Mechanism of Acting

Let us change the focus here from the academics of acting, to the mechanisms of acting. Think of the hundreds of different human characters, that you have met—different in terms of ages, nationalities, accents, and mannerisms. They may look as strange to you as you may look to them. Of all the people we meet in one day, we do not think they all play the same kind of character.

Some may be nice and smart or naive, stupid, cunning, and so on. In terms of concrete acting, or acting to resolve a tension or problem solving, there are the heroes, the villains, and the victims. Yet, I do not think, that we could categorize the whole human population neatly into these three categories. After all, every person has a hero, a villain, or a victim within, that comes out on different occasions. The degree of heroism, villainy, or victimhood may not be the same in everyone. There are people who are predominantly one type in terms of their habits attitudes and values. The more qualities of a hero that one has within, the more of a hero that the person is. That does not simply mean that this person has no attitudes or qualities that make him or her occasionally act like a villain or victim. The same applies for the predominantly villain-like or the predominantly victim-like personalities.

Talking in behavioral terms, there are two kinds of victims: the heroic victims and the villainous victims. Stated differently, the victim can be an incapacitated hero or an incapacitated villain. An incapacitated hero would take the tension out on himself or herself, whereas an incapacitated villain would take it out on others.

There are certain characteristics that go into the making of a hero, a villain, or a victim. In terms of philosophy, the hero would profess, 'live and help live.' The villain would proclaim, 'live and let die.' The pronouncement of the victim, if any, would be 'just live'. Such basic philosophies are gradually formed, as one develops many attitudes, both positive and negative. Most of one's attitudes come from habits, that one is taught or has learned by the influence of parents or the environment. Good habits result in the formation of good attitudes, and bad habits create bad attitudes. An attitude like confidence, for example, is cultivated by a parent who teaches his or her baby to swim at an early age. If good manners are taught and become habits in a child's life, an attitude of respect results, as the child grows older. In the formation of characteristics, attitudes are combined with talents and personality resources, (for instance, one's ability to perceive, conceive, or perform).

Attitudes and talents, along with one's values, determine the mode of acting. Going through each human desire lets us see how a hero, a villain, and a victim go about attainment of his or her desires.

Desire for Food

Food is a biological necessity for life. An infant who would be a future hero, learns to respect food. Eating would be a regulated habit, in terms of the amounts and the intervals. He or she would learn proper eating habits and table manners. He or she would appear graceful and calm while eating meals. Through proper guidance, the child would learn to distinguish between nutritional items and junk food. These habits would transform into attitudes in adolescence. At McDonald's or at home, the teenager would seek a balanced diet. As far as eating goes, an adult hero may look upon the various actions associated with a desire for food, in terms of, nutrition and health first! Sensory experiences of taste, smell, and appearance comes second. Nutrition would be valued as the source for creative energy. Sharing food would be as important to this person as eating. He or she would learn to prepare good meals, and would entertain others as a gesture of friendship.

An infant with villainous traits, may appear aggressive with his meals. He will demand whatever food he likes, whenever he pleases. He will cry and kick until his demand is met, and even if his demand is met, he will steal food from wherever it is stored. In his adolescence, he will develop a selfish attitude toward food. His precedence would be nutrition, but not for creative energy. He would ensure that he is adequately fed even when food is scarce. An adult villain would like to dine in stylish places and entertain guests, often to impress them with a view to influence them for better gains.

A child who's a future victim, would assimilate bad eating habits. He may look desperate while eating his meals. This could be due to starvation or from fear that Mom and Dad would punish him for what he eats or doesn't eat. Begging for food, overeating, and wasting food, are mostly a villainous victim's trait. The baby, who starves and cries for lack of any self-control, is displaying a heroic victim's trait. Such a trait is also displayed by the child, who lacks any interest in food and becomes malnourished. These attitudes become pronounced in adolescence and in adulthood. The victim views food as appealing to his taste and ending his hunger. Either, he is incapable or cannot afford to think about nutrition.

In the order of priorities, food gives a hero energy, health, and sensory satisfaction. Food supplies a villain with pretty much the same, in a selfish way. But for a victim, food is to fill his belly and give him sensory satisfaction. Acts would be devised by all three parties, according to such priorities.

Desires of the Sensorium

An infant, who would be a hero, under parental guidance, and from his own initiative, would proceed cautiously to satisfy the curiosity of his senses, with due respect for the object of his aspiration.

He may gaze at the stars with wonder and admiration, sniff the flowers without plucking them, and run his fingers over his pet dog with care. He couldn't be fussy about the color of his lunch box. In his teens, he discriminates between options with regard to music he listens to, and the shows he watches. He would begin to act more and more like a hero. On reaching manhood, his tastes would become well defined. He begins to relate sensory experiences to certain depths of feelings, which have to do with nature, self, and the people around him. He begins to enhance these experiences, through genuine sharing. He would have a good ear for music and a good eye for art, and he would enhance his talents, by taking up such activities as guitar or painting lessons. He would appreciate the creative talents of others, as much as he would be anxious to share his abilities with others.

For the villainous character, sensation is for self-indulgence? He may share it with others, often to boost his ego, or for a profitable return of some kind. As a child, he is spoiled, and demands sensory enjoyment, regardless of the means of his parents. He acts out a viscous taste for these experiences, by exhibiting the tendencies of a vandal. He likes to look at cartoons filled with violence and mischief. The sounds of firecrackers thrill him. Pulling apart a flower and smearing ice cream over his face are his impulses. As a juvenile, he is into carving out scandalous messages on his classroom desk, playing heavy rock music loudly, despite his neighbor's complaints, drinking and smoking to assert his adulthood, acquiring a thirst for blood, in sports and entertainments, and so on! As a grownup, he acts immaturely, in that, his search for enjoyment and will not have a depth or meaning, other than the attainment of his passions. He will be very eager to display his artistic talents, but he will not be very appreciative of others.

On one extreme, the victim child may disdain sensory experiences. One may not find a twinkle in his eyes when he is presented with a beautiful outfit or a gift. He will not giggle over jingle bells. He is irritable to pampering, and spits out even the most luscious delicacy. During his boyhood, he appears gloomy and disinterested, and he wanders around with an open mouth and an untucked belly. He is preoccupied with self-pity. The full-grown victim in this category, may not have many sensory experiences, because his mind is preoccupied with security, even when he is surrounded by pretty scenes. On the other extreme, the victim child is overwhelmed by sensory experiences and displays a lack of control when eating and drinking.

He becomes completely absorbed by the sights and sounds, to the point of losing awareness of this surroundings, self, and the public. In his absentmindedness, he will become accident prone. He might wander around in his older years, patronizing bars, massage parlors, and casinos with his social security cash. To escape reality, he might smoke and drink to any height or depth.

Thus, the hero indulges in sensory experiences in a respectful manner, the villain acts with disregard for anyone else, and the victim suffers in desperation.

Desire for Affection, Attention, and Acceptance

The heroic baby has a captivating smile. He is not afraid of strangers. He is attentive to your facial expressions, is pleased easily, and shows great patience before crying. His teen years are filled with compliments and admiration from parents and peers. During his high school years, he displays qualities of leadership. He seeks to serve and becomes the president of the student council, and his respect for everyone wins him the election. In time, he gets respect and acceptance from everyone. He gives affection freely and is affected by the concerns and joys of others. As an adult, he expresses gestures of total acceptance, appreciation, and admiration. He listens.

He is thoughtful, open, and sincere. He is kind and helpful. He has a good sense of humor. He shares his possessions and gives gifts. He entertains guests at home. He joins clubs and organizations to enhance friendships. He takes part in humanitarian causes and promotes charity. He becomes a force of love, a center of attraction.

The infancy of a villainous seed is one of belligerence and disobedience. Childish and destructive behavior toward people and property are his game. In his demand for love and attention, he screams aloud. As an older child, he swears at his parents and threatens to hurt them or destroy their belongings, if he does not get his way. In school, he breaks windows, beats up the poor kid, and rides his bike recklessly, to gain the attention of his teachers and peers. Eventually, he settles down and seeks more sophisticated ways of bullying, seeing that his boyish ways would make him a victim in the end. He learns to smile without feelings. He frequently employs flattery and pretense of friendship, to win over anyone he chooses. Others may see him as indifferent, to what they have to say. In pretense of importance, he does not initiate a conversation. He boasts of his resources. He entertains only selected guests, who boost his ego, and have similar tastes. He offers you a cigarette, before borrowing your shirt. If confronted, he becomes extremely defensive. He discredits and intimidates anyone, who appears better or who threatens his interests. In the extreme, he becomes the leader of a gang, involved in the exploitation of the masses, with the ability to bypass the clutches of the law. With these tactics, a villain rises to power in social and political institutions.

To cope with his inadequacies, a victim may resort to heroic or villainous ways of acting, when he needs to get attention. The victim induces sympathy by expressing helplessness, or seeking affection through exhibiting extreme belligerence. As a child, he may have been a crybaby! He may display attention-seeking shyness or animosity. It is hard to please him. At school, he is reclusive, and often gets left out of peer activities and games. He gets picked on, blamed for wrongs, that he has not committed, and is caught easily when he is at fault. By showing up late to school, and by repeatedly forgetting homework (intentionally, or because he is unable to do the work, or because of problems at home), he gets the attention, he does not wish to seek. He lacks the guts to be assertive or speak out. His oversensitivity makes him a victim of ridicule. He is afraid without reason. If there is villainy in him at all, he may show unbiased admiration or flatter his peers, so that he can belong. As he matures into adulthood, he becomes whiney, irritable, and often reclusive. He devalues himself to induce pity from others. He can be evasive about anything. When he is not guilty, he may plead guilty. He may show an inferiority complex. He may openly verbalize his hang-ups. He may threaten suicide or self-harm. If he is really frustrated, he may jump off a bridge. If there is much villainy in him, he becomes a kleptomaniac or even a murderer.

Strategically, the hero seeks affection, attention, and acceptance by giving these qualities freely; the villain by demanding them; and the victim by begging for them.

Desire for Security

In the making of a hero, feeling a sense of security is essential in one's preteen years. To develop a sense of security, the child needs to receive affection, acceptance, and attention from his parents. Children from a loving family are able to easily develop self-confidence. The secret of that self-confidence is the confidence they have in the elders of their family. Such a child begins to show signs of independent thinking. He is able to fiddle around with his toys for long periods of time, without fear that he has been left alone, and without becoming frustrated, that he cannot manipulate his toys, to his heart's content. If he is stuck, he calls for help. Such children do not easily exhibit fear, sadness, worry, great anxiety, or frustration. They are prevented from the prolonged experience of these emotions, by their loving parents. By the time these children reach adolescence, they are grounded in a sense of security; they are ready to survive even in adverse circumstances, with their determination. Success goes their way, when they reach adulthood. The scope of their success depends on their psychological resources. Such adults are alert, careful, and purposeful in their behavior. They constantly set goals. Failure challenges them. Their levels of tolerance are high. They invest money wisely. They carefully pick out careers that suit their personalities. With any frustration they have, they vent through healthy acting, like verbalizing to a friend, and involve themselves in releasing activities. They confront disappointments without losing their cool. Any fortune, honor, prestige, fame, or power that they may accumulate, adds to their security.

The "little devil," or the child with villainous inclinations, may also display the virtue of independence. He may play with his toys quite confidently, but if he is annoyed, he may demolish the toy. His parents might intimidate him, but this will only transform him, into a more rebellious and vindictive personality. If his parents ignore him totally, he will seek to gain security through attention from peers by his bullying behavior. He gets a feeling of security, through smartly manipulating others. He tries to avoid getting caught, and if he does get caught, he tactfully tries to get out of it. He directs his games toward the helpless victims. The grown-up villain ensures his security on material assets, by using whatever personality resources he possesses. He materializes this, through unconventional methods, by cheating on the bureaucratic systems, or by executing his power on such systems, despite any adverse effects, they may bear upon the general public. In any endeavor involving a group or partnership, he ensures his security first and that he would not be handcuffed in a possible disaster. He sets goals and behaves purposefully, giving self-interest full priority. He accepts failures and takes chances, on get-rich-quick ventures. Along with material luxury, he strives for honor, fame, prestige, and power, because these add to his feeling of well-being.

The child who is deprived of affection, attention, and acceptance will lack a sense of security, and will become a victim of either the heroic or the villainous type. Such an infant may trust anybody so innocently, or nobody so dreadfully. The trusting type, in his experiments with material objects, becomes accident prone. He may get slapped around by peers and may grow up with cuts and bruises. He burns the same finger that he's burned twice before. In school, either he is an object of ridicule, or he appears nonexistent. His peers may ordain him as the class fool and may laugh at his inadequate habits and behaviors. Unfortunately, he will be unable to laugh along, because he takes things too personally, thus revealing his helplessness and prompting even more ferocious attacks from peers.

The distrusting type of the victim child, seeks security in shuddering upon the bosom of his mother, on the approach of a stranger. On the spring of his ego, he may hide away to escape embarrassment, or he may become totally evasive. Both the trusting and the distrusting types can grow up to hate the world. Their insecurity would manifest itself in dependence, indecisiveness, incompetence, oversensitivity, feelings of inferiority, inadequacy, and so on or they may lack common sense or may lack goals and purpose in their lives. Laziness, combined with the lack of perseverance and determination, will set them up for failure. They will procrastinate, in whatever they undertake. Their frustrations make them intolerant and irritable. Money matters become disastrous, due to lack of foresight.

Thus, the source of security for the hero is the love that was given to him by his parents, and that he is able to give freely. The villain's source of security is his insurance, and the victim's is neglect. Combined with their personality resources, all of them could achieve different forms and levels of security.

Desire for Appearance, Recreation, and Health

In the vast drama of life, man is born with certain makeups, in terms of facial and physical features, types of hair, complexion, and more. Babies of all ethnic backgrounds are born with certain distinguishing features, that we could call inborn makeups. They may modify or diminish as they grow older.

Makeup (cosmetics) is an essential part of a character on stage. Actors choose appropriate makeups and costumes, that suit the age, the class, and the poise of the characters, that they portray. The clown and the king, the master and the slave, the beggar and the rich, the hooker and the man who buys her—all put on quite becoming makeups willingly, or through customary practices.

In terms of displaying heroic traits, she who prefers to play with the miniature mirror, making faces at her own image, is well, on her way to the philosophy, "Love yourself before you can love others." This child has a positive self-image. If her parents tell her that she is pretty, that is what she sees, every time she looks in a mirror. While in high school, she may put curls in her hair each morning, and may go jogging every evening. She will have vitality in whatever she does, and others will be attracted to his vitality. Appearance is actually the makeup that each individual puts on in the portrayal of one's own character, whether it be clothes, eye shadows, or even certain poise. On the stage of daily living, makeup and costumes are important for the hero, for the successful presentation of the character she is playing, whether it be a school teacher, a policeman, a priest, a nurseor, a cardiologist, or a janitor. It is important to wear what suits one's role, in terms of clothes, makeup, and facial expressions, with a certain sense of honesty. It may not be as appropriate for an army officer to wear a smile on his face at work, as it may be for a social worker. The way one dresses and the way one combs the hair brightens or diminishes the role he is enacting. It gives him confidence in his acting, whatever it is. When one looks the best one can, and if one's looks enhance the depth of the role, it creates a mood of enthusiasm. By definition, the essential features of a hero's makeup would be cleanliness and neatness.

Recreation, whether physical, mental, or spiritual, relieves tension and creates joy in oneself. Play is an act involving physical and emotional expressions, as much as it is a preparation for efficient concrete acting and problem-solving in real-life drama. The man who is active in sports and games seldom seams depressed, simply because he experiences so much relief through play to counteract the tension from living.

Recreation leads to health—physical recreation to physical health, and mental recreation to mental health. Children are induced into play by thoughtful parents, and subsequently play becomes part of their lives. Thus, life becomes enjoyable even when it is serious work. The player can easily seek to perform his role to his best ability, in terms of effective characterization, despite the risks of life's melodramas. If one's playfulness is rooted in purpose and goals, one becomes an achiever in many avenues of life. The fact is that, most professionals and executives are quite athletic and recreation-oriented. They frequently cool off the hot sweat of hard work, through evening sports and entertainments. They get away on weekends and take long vacations. They are into playing chess or cards, attending theatrical performances, taking music lessons jogging, swimming, taking memberships in health spas, and so on, all the while persuing their stressful careers. In the realm of creativity, there are international stars in sports, entertainments, and beauty contests, who maintain a heroic attitude about life.

From infancy to adulthood, the wicked man is conscious of his looks, somewhat like a hero, except that he overemphasizes his appearance and to use it as an ego-boosting mechanism. The infant female may smear makeup from her mother's kit, all over her face, just for a kick. At thirteen, she may try to appear sweet sixteen to ensure that guys will flirt with her. At seventeen, she won't like to keep a steady boyfriend. The infant male may feel an impulse to roll around in daddy's dry-cleaned shirt. He may even give himself a nifty haircut on just one side. At twelve, he may walk around exhibiting machismo, after drinking a can of beer. At seventeen, he may like to appear in a red convertible elevated at the rear with fancy wheels. In adulthood, appearance takes on a new sophistication, in movements and expressions for a villain. Clothes and makeups are chosen to produce the desired devilish impression. The villain needs to appear forceful, like a whirlpool that sucks in, everything around it. He uses his appearance to attract victims. For the villain, recreation is simply excitement, even when it hurts others. The child who smiles while pulling apart an insect, or plays ape in the living room, and the teen who is thrilled at flattening his opponent against the boards in a hockey game, even when the opponent is not carrying the puck, are villainous characters. Such characteristics could later develop a killer instincts. The Romans who threw Christians into the lion's cage, and the Nazis who tortured war prisoners, found a devilish enjoyment in their acts!!!

Health is also a main concern for the villain. It enhances his appearance and vigor, and fulfils his desire to captivate others. The good feeling that goes along with health would be for him, for his own indulgence, rather than cheering up the down-and-out, as it would be for a hero. If he is highly gifted, the villain excels in sports and entertainments and would become a star, not to give out any light, but to bask in the admiration of darkness! As a professional athlete, he caters to the fury of the spectators. In entertainment, he arouses the promiscuous passions of the audience to an extent, where his criminality is overlooked.

The victim may be a dirty child, when it comes to appearance, simply through the negligence of his parents. Consequently, he will be avoided by his family and relatives, except for some superficial gestures of affection. This child may develop a negative self-image in time. He may avoid facing a mirror and may lack interest in personal care. He always feels ugly, after being repeatedly told that he is so, by his folks and friends. This young lad will be afraid to socialize, because of his inferiority complex. Especially in Western society, where attractiveness brings forth a lot of attention, the so-called ugly individuals (whose appearances are often due to neglected personal care) are left out in many circles. Appearance, especially cleanliness, has a lot to do with, acceptance at any age level. The untidy person often gets refused, when seeking a job. His appearance proclaims his underlying attitudes. The recreation of the victim is often limited to drunkenness and inelegant verbalizing. For sensory gratification, he may hang around X-rated movie studios or striptease joints, but he often becomes frustrated after leaving these places, with his aroused passions, and he is further frustrated, by his need to repress such passions. If there is a lot of villainy in this victim, he may end up as a rapist. Ordinarily, he may become depressed over his repression. Health is most often not in the awareness of the victim. He becomes unhealthy, through heavy drinking, smoking, poor eating, and not exercising. His negligent attitude toward appearance, recreation, and health, prepares him to play the role of a perfect victim.

In summary, the hero looks upon appearance, recreation, and health as a means to facilitate his affection and creativity. The villain looks upon these things as means for boosting his ego. The victim usually does not have the time to think of such aspirations, except for giving into cheap thrills.

Desire of Sex

Lust is a passion. Stimulating environments can easily arouse this passion of mankind. Sexual play, in its fundamental form, gives a biological sensation like taste. However, hunger and lust do not have the same biological bases. Desire for food is not just induced by the desire for taste, because food is the fuel for physical and mental energy apart from the cravings of the taste buds. Men have lived without sex, but not without food.

In children, heroic attitudes in terms of discretion toward and respect for sex are primarily directed through parental influences. Even though, sexual impulses, as deep feelings only surface in puberty, the social nostalgia surrounding sex in the milieu of a growing child, surely determines his attitude toward the opposite gender. Teenage sexual behavior is the end product of conflicts between biological urges and parental or social counsel. In terms of displaying heroic behavior, the teenager will try to be respectful and self-disciplined in his interaction with those whom, he finds sexually attractive. He will esteem the human body and human feelings over his sexual passions, and he'll regard sex as a way of expressing love, only in the context of a love relationship. He should try to channel his sexual impulsiveness toward friendship and affection until he finds himself in some perennial love. Then sex will become an expression of love and will be cherished with a special person, with similar feelings. Until that happens, he may seek to relieve his sexual tension, through respectful means. The adult hero's sexual passions will be incorporated into love of one's beloved, and sex will break boundaries, turning passion into blooming romance, assimilating charm, playfulness, fascination, admiration, and kindness. Sexiness will lose its identity in the concept and feeling of love.

There are homes where sexuality is talked about in front of the children by their parents, primarily as entertainment. Such parents may de-emphasize or be indifferent toward fidelity in sexual relationships, both in theory and in practice. They may close their eyes toward the growing tendencies in their children toward sexual exploitation of the vulnerable and the weak. On reaching high school, such villainous characters may participate in sexual mischief. They may ventilate their sexual urges through dirty talk or obscene depictions of sexual promiscuity on public washroom walls. They may make anonymous, obscene phone calls. They may choose to dress seductively and project virility. The sexual passions of the adult villain are far removed from the concept of love. He looks upon women in general, as desirable or undesirable sexual objects. He is often eager to exploit a sexually attractive body, to meet his biological urge for sex, without paying much attention to any deep feelings. He talks about tasty food, expensive cars, and sexy ladies with the same kind of feeling—namely, in objective terms. If he attempts rape, he may use psychological tactics to tame the victim and ensure his security and safety. Female villains may use their sex appeal cunningly to achieve stardom, fortune, and power. In any lasting affair, the villain may look for beauty, youthfulness, cleverness, and money in choosing a partner. He may act peripherally romantic and charming to stimulate such feelings toward him in his sexual partner. Some villains may market sex as merchandise, and they make money through related businesses.

Ignorant or indifferent parent's refusal to instruct a child is partly to blame in cases, where the child developes victim like sexual attitudes. He may fall prey to sexual abuse and, in many instances, develop fear and shame toward his own sexual feelings. Even if not sexually abused, the child may grow up with anxiety over his suppressed sexual feelings. In families where incest exists, especially between children and parents, many children develop great feelings of guilt, that sometimes may last their entire lifetimes. It is usually in puberty, that frustrations related to sex strike the victim. His interpersonal skills are so poor, that he tends to hide from the opposite sex. He may appear gloomy and depressed over his inability to positively channel his sexual desires. If there are traces of villainy in the victim, he may behave irresponsibly with sex. Later he may bear the burden of having to care for a baby and wife, when he is only a teen, and is totally unprepared. If the villainy is much more developed in the victim, he may run away after getting a helpless girl pregnant. Some unwed teenagers and teenage prostitutes often end up as a number in the social assistance sector. In their older years, some may experience several unfulfilling relationships with men, and eventually end up in a world of despair.

In essence, sex for the hero is an expression of love toward his trusted partner. For the villain, sex is a pleasurable experience, and he may not believe in love, in terms of depth of permanence. To the victim, sex is an unrestricted passion, that leaves him without a direction or destination.

Desire for Creativity

It is every man's desire to develop what is within him, and no man is born without some magical talents, however infinitesimal they may be. Inability to develop those typically human aspirations may lead to frustration, and opportunities may not come without challenges. In terms of creativity, the heroic child may begin with imitation and replication of surroundings. He may be curious and observe his surroundings in detail. Besides, the inborn talents that any child may or may not have, parents who are creativity conscious may enroll their children in piano, dancing, swimming, or gymnastic lessons, at the earliest possible age. If both inborn and learned talents are developed, some children may become prodigies in the area of creative arts. In her zeal to develop her potential, she may join the drama or photography club. She may join the swimming or volleyball team of her school. When it comes to academic excellence, children are often encouraged by parents to develop their minds by stimulating them through toys, games, books, and outings to the zoo or a museum. The future hero will always be anxious to learn. Curiosity is the seed of creativity. He may want to dismantle and assemble, modify and simply his objects of study. Destructiveness is seldom his style. He may get through school with straight A's. He may participate in interschool competitions and in general knowledge quizzes.

Children with creative talents in science, art, and sports, enjoy the freedom of their inner souls. With their heroic attitudes, they get attention, recognition, and admiration.

They are the owners of magical charisma. They are special and are liked and loved by many. Everybody has the potential to be creative, but only some achieve stardom. There are two major aspects of creativity. One is talent, both inborn and developed. Essentially, talents are one's physical and psychological resources. Physiological capabilities may get one ready for success in sports and certain aspects of arts. Psychological capabilities like sensory perception, intellectual perception, and awareness of self, surroundings, and others, give one, abilities like observation, curiosity, collection of data, analysis, insight, imagination, and conceptualizing.

Another aspect of success is the right attitudes. These attitudes are enthusiasm, positive thinking, self-esteem, self-discipline, persistence, perseverance, confidence, readiness to take chances when needed, and more. Additional qualities that are typical of a hero are his values. They involve his conduct in fundamental virtues like truth, love, and freedom. He is ethical in his dealings, fair in his relationships, and proud but not arrogant in his accomplishments. Those heroes who have these attitudes and virtues in abundance, plus great creative capabilities, may attain the magnificence of superstardom. The great geniuses in science, music, art, entertainment, sports, and literature will always light up the skies of man's history. Their lights would shine eternally.

As a child, the villain also shows signs of creative potential. But because of his genetic inclinations, parental misguidance, or peer and media influence, he may become deviant in his experiments. In grade five, he may sketch out a plan to blow up the school while the teacher talks about the behavior of certain animals. He may graduate from high school with a notorious ingenuity. It is in certain attitudes and, most importantly, in values that he differs from a hero. He may have many attitudes that make him a success, but he is always clever to find shortcuts. He tries to guard his prestige and ego, and often uses unconventional methods. His stardom may be short-lived. He may remain infamous for some time. May even achieve a momentary superstardom, later to be discredited as an aimless luminary, who collided with history.

Either the victim may have very little creative talent, or may lack the opportunities and attitudes necessary to develop his inherent talents. Let us consider a child of the latter disposition. He will be physically inert, and his mind may be filled with creative urges. He may exhibit occasional excitement when he is filled with creative fantasies. But mostly, he is unhappy in his inability to execute his dreams. He is often neglected and ignored, despite his hidden talents. He may write beautiful poems that express his dreams and miseries, but none will get to read them. His is a loner in school. He may live in the past or in the future, but he seldom in the present. He is frustrated with himself, and may get mad at society at large.

In a hero, the heroic attitudes and values are combined with personality resources to make him creative. In a villain, villainous attitudes and values combine with personality resources brings him success. As for the victim, he may lack the habits, attitudes and values, despite many personality resources, or he may lack all three.

Desire for Honor, Fame, Prestige, Power, and Glory

Often, honor, fame, prestige, power, and glory are complementary terms. They are to be thought of as the ultimate in human desires. Most men are not usually concerned with any of the above, because they are deeply involved in winning the daily bread and gaining financial security. Honor, fame, prestige, power, and glory often follow great accomplishments, except maybe for power, which can come through money. A hero accomplishes these through creativity, love, and a devotion to the truth. Often in the world of sports and entertainment, we are fortunate to see an unusual teenage talent, a mesmerizing power, an extravaganza. Such creative geniuses, glide into glory easily and seemingly, in an instant. In the realm of intellectual endeavors, like scientific discoveries and inventions, the process may be slower and come only after much toil. Such men of distinction will live forever, in the hearts of the human race. Then there are the men of enlightenments, who seek truth and meaning, having conquered their own weakness and having developed great psychic powers. Their lights show us the way through darkness into the serenity and divinity, that they have accomplished. We call them the holy men, the prophets, the savior, the messiah, and so on.

The ideology of the villain is that, material and social power will give him honor, fame, prestige, and glory. He is determined to attain power through psychological manipulation of the masses. His emergence into fame and glory will be quite sensational, and he knows that the average man is overwhelmed by sensationalism. He may use his power to exploit humanity, and lead people into subversion. Many a civilization has been destroyed by villains, who have misled their devoted followers.

To the victim, honor, prestige, fame, power, and glory are unthinkable. Glory might have been possible for the victims, when innocence was thought to be one of the highest virtues, if and when one could have been canonized, by virtue of one's immaculate innocence. But today, the victim's only hope for fame, and maybe for some strange kind of temporary glory, is through bizarre acts like mass killings, the attempted murder of a VIP, or a suicide committed in some strange setting. For a victim to do any of these, he has to have a high degree of villainy in him.

A heroic victim would take only his own life, and only in secrecy. A victim who dares to be vicious may have the maddening desire to be acknowledged, one way or another. In the end, he would only be acknowledged as a victim, who exploded with rage, toward the society from which he felt excluded.

Actors and Acting

An Actor Is Born

We already discussed babies of different ethnic origins, being born with distinguishing features. Regardless of ethnic origin, babies do differ in their acting and reacting, even when they are reared in environments that are similar. Babies still in the cradle generally act and react in accordance with their physical comforts, needs, and the affection and attention they are given. Their eyes light up in comfort and companionship, and go dim in discomfort and loneliness. Some babies, maybe due to physical causes, are naturally irritable, lethargic, and more easily displeased, than others. Most babies are a delight to watch, as they roll their eyes, show their gums, and throw punches at you, in sheer playfulness, often accompanied by strangled sounds of glee.

Not all babies are the same kind of actors, when it comes to crying, laughing and being active. Things may or may not change as they attain more mobility and learn more actions. A lot depends on the milieu in which they modify their actions, as well as the kinds of assistance they receive.

The Actor Is Formed

Love and lack of love can be considered as presenting the force of good, and the force of evil, respectively. The feelings associated with love are affection, acceptance, attention, kindness, respect, trust, honesty, conscientiousness, confidence and happiness. The feelings associated with the lack of love are hatred, anger, fear, sadness, loneliness, worthlessness, despair, greed, and selfishness.

Any of the feelings associated with lack of love may attack one fiercely. Such emotional attacks will bypass rational thinking, or the awareness of the self, and it may impact of one's actions upon others. Thus, a sudden rage or fury is an emotional attack, that leaves one blindfolded in terms of insight. Children are vulnerable to such emotional attacks, in varying degrees. Some children are short-tempered due to biological causes or aggravating adults. Many of us may recall childhood temper tantrums that resulted in destructive and dangerous acting out. Some people may gain more control over their impulsiveness, with age, and some do not. The destructive power of the adult fury is greater than that of the infant fury, just as war between countries are more destructive than tribal wars. Repeated outrages of deep feelings or passions in which one loses his self-awareness and self-control, may lead to maladjustment or abnormal acting.

Let us get back to love and lack of love, the good and the evil, the fundamental principles of good acting and bad acting. Starting with the child, one has to receive love before one is able to give it. She has to receive it from the adults and peers around her, as she grows older. If she is provided with her physical needs, and given affection, attention, and acceptance, and at the same time, she is praised for her good acts and told of the unacceptability of her bad acts, then she will develop a healthy and positive personality. This child will mature into a hero, and her acting will be colored with respect, kindness, honesty, trust, and confidence.

Hatred and anger are produced in a child, when her physical needs are not met, when she is not given enough affection or acceptance, and when the attention she receives is only given while she is doing the wrong things. Because she needs attention so badly, and because doing the right things never gets attention for her, she makes it a habit of doing the wrong things. Consequently, everybody hates her, and she hates everybody. This is the story of belligerence. This child will become either a villain or a victim. Lack of love is at the root of all bad attitudes, whereas love is at the root of all good attitudes.

If the villain gets his acceptance, attention, and physical comforts through exploitation, the original hatred and anger will transform into cruelty and covetousness. In the case of the victim, the original hatred and anger will turn into despair, fear, and guilt.

Fear and guilt are conditioned feelings. If a child's parents make him frightened of the dark, of water, of strangers, or of ghosts, the child may develop phobias as years go by. Yet, threatening children with punishments of hellfire, when a child does wrong, can induce a feeling of guilt in that, the child 'feels guilty' without reason, or who is constantly critical of himself. Oversensitivity is another possible effect of such an upbringing.

Hatred, anger, and fear grow, where love is lacking, and they create villains and victims. Villains acclaim social acceptance by bending the rules, and they even make the rules to protect themselves. Victims, with the severity of their problems, can collapse into psychological rubbish, filled with anger, anxiety, fear, guilt, and sadness!

Anger, anxiety, fear, guilt, and sadness are at the roots of most neurotic and psychotic behaviors, except for the ones, that are organically based. The victims are of two kinds: the heroic and the villainous, the ones who take it out on themselves, and the one who blames on others. The heroic victims may be maladjusted and act depressed, phobic, obsessive, compulsive, suicidal, or alcoholic. He could even become homicidal or psychopathic.

Where there is love, there is forgiveness. With forgiveness comes peace. Forgiveness takes understanding of self and others. One has to learn to forgive oneself and others in order to find peace. By accepting the past and the present and forgiving one's self and the other, one can find everlasting joy.

The Actor Chooses a Role

All living beings are adaptive. Adaptation is a survival mechanism. Basically, adapting is more reacting than acting in subhuman species. In man, the adapting and coping mechanisms, are highly developed. Man may be a product of his environment until he develops his awareness of the self. When or to what degree one develops self-awareness, in terms of knowing one's strengths and weaknesses, varies. Regardless of age, talents can be enhanced, and attitudes and values can be changed. Then, why do some people try to change, and others do not! Change begins with the awareness of one's milieu, one's self, and others with whom one deals with. Also, change is the end product of many little changes. It is not accomplished overnight. Other factors influencing change, are willpower, determination, influence by others, books, philosophies, education, or even catastrophes, and the like.

I believe that there is a part in the brain that has to do with awareness. What triggers awareness, could be thoughts of awareness or thoughts on awareness, when one is preoccupied with the meaning of life. Awareness could be triggered from one's childhood years, when one is taught to examine the self. Many religious sects encourage such periodical self-evaluation. This can be negative and harmful, if one is to develop terrible feelings of guilt, under rigid religious doctrines, where the concept of sin is overemphasized. Not having any self-evaluation, however, is more destructive and dangerous. If self-evaluation is based on positive attitudes and positive values, personal growth is the outcome: one may learn to correct negative attitudes and values, and may develop positive altitudes and values. Then there are people who develop awareness later in life, by virtue of the influence of other people, or an appealing philosophy. There are different degrees of awareness. The more aware one is of his milieu, own strengths, and weaknesses, as well as the way society is, the more is his potential for change. But then, awareness alone does not make the change. It takes determination or willpower.

Determination or willpower also can be a conditioned attitude, taught through the work of inspiring parents and teachers. Change is impossible without developing an attitude of determination, especially when one is stubborn and his habits and attitudes are set. To get his power of will, one has to contemplate his bad habits and ardently desire a change. Determination for change may come from the influence of others, books that one may read, or philosophies one may encounter. Such influences can inspire one, only if he is exposed to them and is receptive.

Education is a big factor in change, and grownups can be influenced to change as well as children. If one is presented with the facts about the nature of things, positive change is a desirable outcome. One's concept of reality becomes fuller and more encompassing, when one has the knowledge in as many different areas as possible. There are series of misfortunes and catastrophes that may get one in touch with one's deepest self. Stories of change following bad events are told by many every day.

Whatever the cause of change may be, after going through periods of confusion, many adults decide on a specific character, that they want to portray at home and at work. In day-to-day interactions, most people play a role or character without completely revealing themselves. Different people reveal their inner selves to others, to different degrees. A total revelation may occur in an intimate friendship. In today's society, one does not have to reveal the self at any level. It is one's performance that counts. That best performer is the "best actor" in everybody's eyes. The incentive for performance for some people is security; for others, it is affection, attention, and acceptance. For some, the motivation is creativity, for others it is money, power, prestige, honor, fame, and glory. The quality and honesty of one's performance depends on the kind of incentive or desire he is after.

The Sum and Substance of Acting

Let me summarize, in the form of equations, the different combinations of ingredients that mix in the making of heroes, villains, and victims.

Talents + positive attitudes + positive values = hero Limited talents + positive attitudes + positive values = hero Talents + certain positive attitudes + positive values = hero

Talents + certain positive attitudes + negative values = villain Limited talents + certain positive attitudes + negative values = villain

Talents + negative attitudes + positive values = heroic victim Limited talents + negative attitudes + positive values = heroic victim

Limited talents + negative attitudes + negative values = villainous victim

As indicated in the equations, regardless of talents, attitudes, and values, one can determine the heroism, the villainy, and the victimhood in anybody. Talents only determine the sphere and extent of activity for the three groups. The essential characteristics of a hero are positive habits, positive attitudes and positive values; the villain has certain positive attitudes but also negative values; the victim has negative attitudes regardless of his values or abilities.

Even if one is born to play the role of a victim in view of a particular upbringing, one does not have to stay that way. To change the victim into a hero, the first thing to be worked out is his attitude. Confidence, persistence, perseverance, competence, tolerance, optimism, patience, and pride are the attitudes that a victim may lack. Inculcating such attitudes in an adult is difficult to do. If children are instructed in positive attitudes through teaching of good habits and correcting of bad habits, a healthy growth of personality is possible. The educational system is the only effective instrument that can bring about such changes in today's morbid society, with its changing family structures.

As important as the attitudes are the values. Positive values like truth, love, and freedom are heroic, whereas negative values like dishonesty, self-centeredness, and oppression are villainous. Regardless of the philosophical and religious beliefs, good values are valuable for any hero.

If habits and attitudes are founded on the positive basic human values of truth, love, and freedom, a healthy personality results. Even though hard work is a good habit, workaholics often disregard physical and mental health. Even if sensitivity is good for man, oversensitivity paralyzes one, making one incapable of any constructive action. Some guilt over bad habits is healthy, because it serves to correct these habits. But a guilty conscience cripples a person, making one feel helpless and depressed.

The Plot

What could be the plot of this extravaganza called life? What is the story of the human drama? I believe that there are three themes to our life story: love, freedom, and truth.

The stage, the earth itself, can be thought as being made of love. The material world, the plant kingdom, and the animal kingdom are the result of inorganic and organic particles working together. In subatomic particles coming together to form elements and compounds, we can see some basic principles of love (i.e., affiliation and partnership). The same principles are at the core of the living species. The cells in a living organism are interdependent and mutually assist one another.

Thus, the stage is made of material particles that come together to form the land, the waters, the air, the plants, and the animals. These things furnish the scenic details on earth. They are all linked together by interdependency. Animals depend on plants, plants depend on animals, and they both depend on soil, water, and air.

Love itself is one of the themes of human life. From a tribal society to the metropolitan culture, men have depended on one another and looked to one another for support and subsistence. From the relationships, in one's own family to the international interdependency, it has always been a story of mutual assistance and affiliations, however unfriendly men may have become to one another, at times.

Another theme of the human drama is freedom—that is, developing the potential in nature and self. Man has come a long way in overcoming his many limitations. However, he has a long way to go in overcoming his weaknesses, which stand in the way of expressing his creative talents and enjoying the feeling of freedom.

Truth is the other theme of life. Finding facts about the world and the self has been one of man's prime preoccupations. This has enhanced his freedom and his horizons of creativity. He has always searched for the meaning of existence, and the search will continue in the future.

The following chapters will deal with love, freedom, and truth, the three themes of this extravaganza called life.

2

TO HEAVEN
WITH LOVE

Love is a value, a fundamental principle of life. Many positive attitudes and habits develop from love. Positive attitudes like tolerance and altruism are merely ramifications of the fundamental value of love. Only love can hold the world together. All laws, natural and man-made, are simply expressions of the law of love.

But what is love? How can we define love? It would have been easy, if love were an entirely objective phenomenon. However, there is no reason why we shouldn't tie in the objective laws, the laws governing the material world, with the law of love. Atomic particles attract one another, forming a variety of substances essential for life. Living organisms, including man, have a passion for material things, whether it be, air, food, or an object of beauty. Living organisms themselves interact invariably. Taking all these into account, we could define love as a dynamic experience of fulfillment among subjects through objective and subjective media. Therefore, love is a cosmic affair.

Subjects in the generalized sense include God and man. Love, then, is the creative and endless interaction between God and man. The objective media are material things, plants and animals. Here, plants and animals are included under objective media for convenience. They could well be considered as subjects by virtue of their psychic endowments.

The Objective Media

The Biggest Accident!

Sharing material things essential for life, is an activity that establishes that relationship of fulfillment in individuals. Before we discuss this point in detail, it is important to undermine this fascination of ours towards matter.

Where does matter come from? Scientists might tell us that the answer is somewhere in the galaxies. While they watch the clusters of stars though powerful telescopes and analyze the data to find out the physics and chemistry of the origin of matter, we have no way of concluding anything about the source of matter. If we accept the big bang theory and the resultant primordial expansion, we have to come with a starting point for the creation of this universe.

In the sixth century BC, the Milesian school of philosophers of ancient Greece believed that the universe was formed as a result of a series of natural, rather than supernatural, events. The Pythagorean school of the same era supported this belief, with a concept of the universe as governed by certain mathematical principals. The modern scientific speculations, on the origin and evolution of the universe, were initiated in 1929 by a discovery of US astronomer Edwin Hubble that the galaxies were moving away from one another. This discovery, together with Einstein's theory of general relativity, laid the foundations of modern cosmology. In 1965, US physicists Arnold A. Penzias and Robert W. Wilson discovered background blackbody radiation, thereby supporting the big bang hypothesis.

The energy released during the process of primordial explosion is believed to have transformed into the radiation that was detected in 1965 by the US physicists. There is substantial evidence today that thermonuclear reactions and explosions within stars generate the chemical elements and distribute them in the interstellar space from which new generations of stars and planets are born. Whatever be the case, the missing piece of the puzzle is the origin of matter and antimatter. They cannot come from nothing, because something cannot come from nothing. What could be the source of the energy of the universe? So far, science cannot give us any definite answers. It has nothing yet to say about the source of matter, or the essence from which the primordial particles arose. A universe may start from a very concentrated energy beyond understanding. Here is where we have to look outside of the realm of telescopes and galaxies and search for answers from other sources.

If you are a theist, the simple answer that God created the universe would satisfy your quest. If one is ready accept this starting point, one could ask oneself, "How did God create the universe?" The six-day story of creation was written for a people whose mental age was very low. But the message of that story could be good enough for any generation that God is the creator, and that there is a well-directed ascending evolutionary sequence, from matter to man. Traditional theologians and religious philosophers, out of great respect for the omnipotence of God, propagated the idea that God created the world out of nothing. When increasing scientific data contradicted the literal interpretation of the Bible, some scientists showed eagerness to deny the existence of God.

At any rate, the design and pattern of the galaxies and stars are really something to think about. Most of us cannot afford to go to La Palma, Spain, to view the galaxies and stars through 'the Gran Telescope', the largest telescope in the world, but a trip to the nearest planetarium will do magic!. It is amazingly beautiful to look at the mysteries lying beyond our natural vision. Appreciating the beauty, the pattern, and the power of objects of this magnitude, is crucial for our relationship of love with the Creator. The respect, gratitude, admiration, and affection toward God that results from contemplating the magnificence and magnitude of his creation, would enable man to realize that he is part of this phenomena, and is fortunate enough to have a complex brain, that can explore the endless possibilities for his comfort and convenience. As it is, even without the recognition of man, the universe is beautiful.

When matter cools on the surface of the planets, the subatomic particles become so unsettled that they search for a security and coherence in a unit of an atom. It is a fairly stable and satisfying relationship. However, it doesn't stop there. Atoms like to grow by making friends with other atoms out of mutual respect and without destroying each other, sharing their electrons and assuming a multitude of shapes, patterns, and colors. Whether atoms join with their own kind to form elements, or with other kinds to form compounds, their creative relationship adds to the beauty of our planet, and is suggestive of a lot of things about the relationship of animals and humans. The result of this atomic and molecular interaction, adds beauty to nature, with such materials like silver, gold, and diamonds, and it provides the environment with plenty of natural resources, for organisms to live in harmony. The physical energy, directly or indirectly vital for the metabolism of plants, animals, and men, has to come from soil. Life owns its pulse to the air, water, and minerals that sustain it. Living is a precondition for loving. Next, we will look at the laws of the material world that have made living and loving easy for us.

They Physics and Chemistry of Matter

Upon examining an atom, we can find many basic scientific principles. The opposing charges of the protons and electrons, the revolution of electron around the nucleus, the radiant energy inherent in the nucleus, and so on, are basic principles, similar to the greater scientific laws of the universe. If we say that these principles came about in the atom through some special properties, of the subatomic particles. what is the source of such special subatomic properties?

The complexity of the structure of matter, and galaxies and the mechanisms of the activities of matter, are not man-made mysteries. Scientists only discover the natural principals, which they then use to promote comfortable living. Even before Copernicus discovered that the sun was the center of the solar system, or Newton discovered why the apple would not fall upward to the sky, these principals existed. Mechanics, thermodynamics, magnetism, electricity, optics, nuclear physics, and quantum mechanics are names for the principals, governing the universe, which the human brain has been struggling to uncover. Are they all accidental mechanisms, or is there a master brain behind them, organizing these systems so brilliantly? There are many scientists who are reluctant to talk about it. It is a fact that even the most complicated computers will never be as good as the human brain, or that the brilliant design of a faultless jet plane will only be a cheap imitation of flying organisms.

The dazzling colors that compose the sunlight and the chemical properties that absorb and reflect the various components of the spectrum have worked together to give us landscapes filled with an array of colors and designs. Here also, man has used the principals behind the physics and chemistry of colors and textures to make more objects of beauty. Advances in inorganic, organic, analytical, applied, biological, and physical branches of chemistry make use of the basic principles, inherent in the relationships of atoms and molecules. Hereditary factors like DNA and RNA are not man-made, although with experimentation, man might be able to control hereditary limitations and increase human potential. Another point to consider is the development of the human brain itself. If the brain in man developed through evolution, why do we use only less than 10 percent of it? The rest may eventually become functional as we gradually make use of it. But the rest of the brain is already there. To think that man developed all of his brain, is illogical. The human brain should be thought of as the creation of, a higher power.

If love is the dynamic experience of fulfillment between subjects, how do soil and plants fit in as media for this? First, let us take into consideration the fulfillment of the subjects. This individual fulfillment of the necessities of life, as I mentioned before, is a prerequisite for fulfillment of the subjects. The undeveloped subject, plant thrives on, fertilizers from the soil. It is a self-sacrifice in a primordial sense for the atoms of the soil to lose their identities so that plant life may serve other species in a similar way. To lose one's life to serve another has always been considered an act of love. In the case of matter, even though there is no life to lose, a change of identity and an active participation in activities within the plants are definitely an act of total giving.

As the animal species attained more and more complexity, man finally came on the earth. The earth's usefulness changed from a source of fuel alone, to a source of sensory experience. It was as if the earth was saying, "Live and love through me." Man discovered that he could stretch, shrink, and mold matter into any color and any shape, and for any use. Thus, he made color televisions, sports cars, and dazzling clothes. Material media serves as a tool for love when we use material objects to establish that creative and dynamic relationship between subjects. The other side of the token is that matter can be used for opposite ends too. Make it into a nuclear weapon, and you have the tool for the termination of life. In the evolutionary process, the plant kingdom did not get anywhere in terms of complexity and consciousness. It is as if plants were assigned a specific and everlasting job, without any promotion. They were put into the service of animals and humans. Plants do not bear fruits to feed their own offspring, but to feed us. The shape, color, and taste of the fruits make them tempting for man and animals. Plant life is fulfilled by being enjoyed by other species. They feed our lungs with oxygen that they generate, our eyes with green fields, flowers, tall trees, and landscapes, our bodies with shade, breeze, and shelter, our bellies with vegetables and fruits, our nostrils with aroma from flowers, and our ears with whistling sounds. Do we appreciate the kindness of plants enough? If we do, we have to learn to plant a tree before we chop one down.

The animal kingdom has an equally important role in supporting our lives. The design of the ecosystem is such that the creative fulfillment can be achieved only through respectful interaction of all forms of life. The way things are today, not too many people think it immoral to eat meat. Killing to survive is part of the norm for creatures, including man. Mohandas Gandhi, who was the leader of the struggle for India's independence, considered meat eating cruelty toward animals. To him, it was wrong to take life except for plants, even if it was to sustain another life. The man who kills animals has it all wrong. Animals have senses. They can feel the sharpness of a butcher's knife just as man can. Furthermore, vegetation can provide enough nourishment for any life, and the plant is not hurt by picking the beans or plucking the leaves. Plants do not have a center of consciousness, as animals do.

Most of us are not about to give up eating meat because of this argument. Is there any justification for being a non-vegetarian? I guess we have to answer that question by asking ourselves what the purpose of existence is for each state or form of creation. The major function of matter and plants is to act as a source of energy for man and animals. It is a self-sacrifice in which they attain their fulfillment. It could be argued that animals have a similar function when it comes to the survival of man. The advocates of vegetarianism would not agree. They would say that plant food is better for our health, and that we could get enough of it, if only we desire it.

For man, love is difficult without the help of soil, plants, and animals. We get the nutritional energy from them, for our activities. We also get the fuel for the industrial productivity from nuclear and solar energy sources, as well as coal and oil. Coal is from the trees that lived a long, long time ago, and that were buried under the soil to be ready for our use. The micro-organisms that died by the billions under the sea years and years ago have given us oil, the precious fluid of the industrial world.

Sharing Is Caring

All men crave material things. The media promotes the doctrine of getting things in order to make ourselves and our immediate family comfortable, as opposed to giving away to someone, who desperately needs things. It is easy to wash one's hands by saying that decisions are made for us by the manufacturers of necessity, luxury, or entertainment items. We have to admit that most of our society is more conditioned than autonomous. Our decisions could act as media for interpersonal relationships, if only we evaluated them in terms of the interests of the whole human family. I am not suggesting that such an evaluation is necessary for each decision. It is the attitude that counts. A man who is concerned about the needs of others cannot be too narrow-minded to be overly possessive. A country that harkens to the cry of the starving cannot dump food away to balance the economy.

Some of the most generous people in the world live in North America. They give away enormous quantities of wheat and milk powder to feed millions of hungry people around the world. But the younger generation seems to be less generous in this "brave new world" that urges them to get ahead by any means. It is a fact that a dollar bill, which is insignificant for many of us, could buy as much as a week's groceries for someone on the other side of the globe.

Organizations like the Salvation Army and UNICEF are good vehicles within which to utilize one's urge to give. People in general have the tendency to throw away unwanted items like clothes or furniture, unaware that, there are hundreds of others, whose lives would be easier, if people took the time to give things away.

Sharing takes place every day in our homes. Parents and children, husbands and wives, friends and neighbors—all share material objects to express their love. Giving is the most important expression of love. Receiving is actually reciprocal giving. The one who gives is bound to receive. Even without the receiving part, giving itself is a joyous act for a loving heart. Living has no meaning if it is not a basis for loving. That is a lesson we have to learn from the material world and the plant and animal kingdom.

The Subjective Media

Man the Lover

Whatever the religious and secular speculations may be on the origin of life, living organisms thrived in the comforts of nature, increasing in complexity and consciousness, except for the plant kingdom. Before the biosphere became equipped with sensory mechanisms, nature remained a song unsung, a beauty unseen. Not only the senses but the three faculties of the psyche,(body, mind and spirit), are essential for experiencing life to the fullest. As the sensory faculty extracts pleasures from the material world, intelligence is needed to invent, and consciousness is needed to be conscientious.

The sensory apparatus, with organs like the eyes, ears, tongue, and nose, as well as their connections in the brain, are designed so brilliantly that we cannot comprehend exactly how the messages are translated into notions, thoughts, and insights. Even the most complicated cameras are nothing compared to the eye. If man invented artificial eyes, they would be operational only with the help of the brain. Hearing, smelling, and touching also involve very complicated sensory systems.

Let us imagine, that the computer technology one day came up with a robot, with all the sensory organs, and it was hooked up to an artificial brain capable of emotional experiences and critical analysis. Could there be a community of such robots without the intervention of man? It seems most unlikely. Man is much more than his visible structure, with all its complicated systems. Just as the computer needs a programmer, the physical structure is functional only as long as the psyche pervades it.

The Passion for Love

By polarizing the functions of the senses, we could say that senses act as the media for living, when they satisfy the bodily needs of the individual, and they act as the media for loving, when they satisfy his spiritual needs, to share, care, and be involved. But it is difficult to draw a line between living and loving, because all our activities involve others directly or indirectly. Most of the items that we use for daily living are the products of labor of other people. The farmer who produces the potatoes for us, or the textile worker who produces our clothes, might not be aware of it, but what he does is an act of love. Here again, attitude is the determining factor; he might be working just for the money. Objectively speaking, it still an act of love, although subjectively it is not.

Beauty and the Beast

Of all sensory experiences, perhaps sight is most precious. Mountains and valleys filled with colorful trees and f lowers, oceans and lakes fluttering with waves and sand, glittering in the sunlight, parks and museums teeming with life—all fulfill our sense of sight.

Deriving inspiration from the environment, man has been able to create beauty through artistic efforts in various media. Even though the bird's nest, the bee's honeycomb, or the spider's web have artistic enchantment, each has always done it the same way. But with man, techniques are always changing. The carved stones of primal man were only the beginning. History produced great men like Michelangelo and da Vinci, who will always be immortal for their artistic perfections.

Technology has given modern art an entirely new face. Photography today, for instance, is able to produce pictures and movies more vivid and colorful than before. Commercial artists can mass-produce items of beauty. Toys, clothes, and cars have an increasing variety of styles and appearances. Some of the modern architecture project an outer-space image.

The criterion of creativity is the usefulness of the object of creation for personal growth and interpersonal relationships. However, beautiful objects could inspire one with greed, rather than toward using them to consolidate lasting and respectful relationships.

Visual experiences, especially in entertainment, can have personalizing or depersonalizing effects. They can inspire man to love his fellow being. They can also provoke his negative attitudes and deprive him of his ability to care and respect. Unfortunately, many of the shows today are based on the philosophy that sensationalism makes money, especially if it is geared toward the weakness of man.

The Sound of Music

Sound is an ineffable sensory experience, and music is one of the most popular and inexpensive entertainments in the world. Its therapeutic effect on our labored minds after a strenuous day is magical. It uplifts our spirits and steals away our worries. The rhythm and melody of music can permeate our spirits and bodies so that we feel like dancing to the tune. Parties and nightclubs would not be so alive without it.

The cavemen who sat around a fire singing songs of praise about their gods, or about the heroism of their ancestors, derived a feeling of confidence and unity. In the course of time, the themes of songs changed. They became about day-to-day problems, adventure, and everlasting love.

Music is a powerful medium that can either invoke us to reach out to our neighbors in love or infatuate us to seek selfish pleasures. The words in the music, which we call lyrics, are very important in formulating the human personality, especially in the teenage years. Long ago, love and peace were everything that we could sing about. Today, many songs celebrate passion for sex without principles.

The most important function of sound is communication, which involves talking and listening. Communication is inevitable for socialization and relationships. Even if communication is possible without words, verbal dialogue makes it easier. The personality of a person is reflected in the way he talks. Attitudes and interests of an individual come out through his talk. But beware of sweet-talkers; beware the hooks behind the bait.

The human tongue is the greatest of all weapons. It can make or break friendships, create or destroy societies, and enslave or free the world. We often hear the sayings "Watch your language" or "Watch what you say." Intelligence can twist tongues tactfully for good or bad.

Speaking and listening are complementary to each other. Communication should be listening more than talking. Misunderstanding and misjudgment are the results of inadequate listening. In the free world of ours, the urge to talk more often dominates the willingness to listen. Communication between parents and children and husbands and wives, would be meaningful only if what one has to say reflects the interests, needs, and self-actualization of all parties involved.

A Smell of Roses

In making flowers attractive, nature furnished them with colors and scent. Fresh air filled with the fragrance of nature is always energizing. Nature has its own ways of enriching the air with oxygen, in order to provide us with the breath of life so that our cells can produce the energy we need for activities. The perfumes and colognes that we make in laboratories are synthesized from the crude products of nature. Pollution and unpleasant odors that clog up or nostrils and contaminate our lungs are man-made menaces. The dizziness and fatigue caused by the factory, the city, and cigarettes always get us down. There are two solutions to the problem: either we can get away, or we can investigate ways to improve the situations.

Establishing industrial and residential zones away from each other, increasing recycling processes, and encouraging people to dispose of waste properly would be the concerns of a scrupulous man.

A Taste of Honey

From the raw meat and wild honey of the caveman to the barbecued steak and banana splits of the city man—how our tastes have changed! Nature is filled with a good supply of tasty foods, and man knows how to cook them. Each country has developed its own techniques to make food delicious. Sugar and spices work miracles on our appetite, even to the point of forcing us to forget nutritional values. An apple, an orange, or a pineapple is not only great tasting, but it's good-looking as well. On top of it, our biological nature has given us an appetite that increases the desire for food. Under the right conditions, eating is a pleasurable experience to everyone.

Eating is not just for the enjoyment of it, although enjoyment makes eating easier. Today in America, more than ever, there is great emphasis on nutrition. We have begun to talk about health foods and the nutritional values of our daily menus. Researchers in the area link not only physical but also psychological health to the foods we consume. Food is man's fuel for physical and mental activities. Man is no different from cars in this respect. Regardless of the make of the car, impure gasoline can ruin the engine; with man, garbage food can damage physical and mental health.

Chemical preservatives and additives and artificial sweeteners are coming under investigation, to see their physiological effects. Studies on saccharin have proven it to be a cancer-causing ingredient when administered to certain animals. Chlorine in our drinking water is an item of suspicion. Synthetic food and preservatives, if not thoroughly tested, could have dangerous physical and psychological impacts on future generations. It would be nice if we could solve a lot of our problems with the use of chemicals and chemistry. But if they are going to create for us more complicated problems in the future, then we better proceed with caution.

Many nations in the European Union have done great revisions on food-packing regulations. Synthetic colors are being tested and used with precaution. In 1975, the US Food and Drug Administration imposed restrictions on using polyvinyl chloride (PVC) in packaging food due to the possibility of carcinogenic concerns. Controversy over the FDA's role as a mediator between consumer and producer has put much pressure on the organization to revise its activities and have more consumer protections.

While men and women in developed countries spend large amounts of money on weight-control programs, in many developing nations being overweight is a sign of luxury and financial boom. Children in the Western world are raised on chocolate bars and thus have an affinity toward sweets all their lives. Experiments show that children can be conditioned to be less desirous of sweets if the quantity of sugar is reduced in baby food. Obesity is never a reason for abstaining from sweets, unless one is rational about it. We sometimes forget that the primary function of food is to fuel us, and eating anything at any time will skyrocket our blood pressure. Rational men eat to live and live in health. Waste of food or overconsumption is a crime, when starvation is a serious world problem. Love could begin with breaking the bread on our table at suppertime, but it should not end there. There are people in the developing world, who are far from well fed and need a few slices from us.

The Touch of Love

To touch and to be touched is a craving that man has from birth to death. Touching is an expression of the need to love and to be loved. Regardless of age, physical contact is one of the most intimate ways to express love. A hug from a mother can make a child forget all his worries. A smile and the gentle touch of a nurse can cure half the disease of the patient. A kiss and words of love can make a lover sensitive and sentimental. We all long for a gentle touch and kind words at times. The healing power of touch is miraculous. It can give us confidence, make us forgive, and bring out the best in us.

Let us now look at the sexual aspects of human relationships. Sexual intimacy, and intercourse in particular, can be one of the most fascinating ways to express love. The Adams and Eves of the human race perhaps did not quite understand the relationship between sex and childbirth. To them, perhaps, sex was the result of physical attraction and conjugal instincts. To the early man, menstruation and childbirth were incidents controlled by the gods, with no connection to the phenomenon of sex itself. Then times changed. The ancient Greeks and Romans, even though understood the connection between sexual intercourse and pregnancy, emphasized the sensual aspect of sex. Different methods were used for birth control, thus stressing the entertainment value of sex. Hebrews, especially with the introduction of the Ten Commandments, sanctioned sex as a privilege only for couples in love, with love being certified and sanctified in the institution of matrimony. Fornication and adultery were held in great contempt.

Christ, being a celibate himself, emphasized the serious and sacred nature of sex. To him, fornication and adultery were the selfish expressions of a desire to use others for pleasure and therefore were acts of sin and deterrents of love.

Christ's celibacy has to be understood in terms of the social and technological standards of his time. With very little mechanization, manual labor was the only means for sustaining a family. It took days for them to do the work we do in minutes and hours. Raising a family was a full-time occupation, and there was very little time to devote to the problems of the community. To Christ, perhaps being a celibate was the only way for carrying out his mission, which was a serious challenge to the monarchy and moral standards of his time. The priestly celibacy that followed in the Catholic Church has to be understood in this context. Self-imposed celibacy is valid only if it becomes a means for enlarging the horizons of love, enabling someone to reach out to more people more readily in more ways. A celibate has the advantage of not being tied down by time he would devote to his wife and children. In a missionary endeavor that demands a lot of one's time and dedication, especially when one has to live for long periods of time in secluded areas with very little mechanization, no schools, and few conveniences for the family, a celibate might be better equipped. In the past, it was definitely so.

Marriage is a means of love, as much as celibacy is. A married minister can be as much humanitarian as a celibate monk, especially in the modern world. Credit has to be given to anyone who can take up the responsibility of a family and at the same time devote himself to the service of God. In application, the lifestyle does not matter as long as the commitment is there. Being a celibate is not easy, especially in the Western world. In a society in which sex is merchandised as popular adult entertainment, and the environment and the media are filled with an air of sensuality to the extent of idolizing it in place of the traditional values, a celibate priest might find it difficult to not be tempted unless he is filled with the spirit of commitment to bring people to God. Celibacy, for the sake of total dedication to one's fellow beings, has to be considered as an act of self-sacrifice. Not everyone has the psychological makeup to undertake it.

In our sensuous era, more than ever, man has the tendency to equate love with sex. Sex need not always be a medium for love. A rapist uses sex as a weapon, a prostitute uses it for money, and a playboy uses it for pleasure. Sex in these cases has nothing to do with love. To elaborate this point further, a distinction has to be made between liking and loving; liking is an objective phenomenon, whereas loving is subjective. They do not contradict each other, and neither can they be completely separated. Yet a distinction has to be made because liking cannot be a universal condition or criteria for loving. Liking is the result of craving of our senses. On the material level, flowers, food, music, perfumes, and soft cushions appeal to our eyes, tongue, ears, nose, and physical sensitivity. In the case of man, the way one walks, talks, and smiles might compel another to like him or her. Physical beauty in one's partner is something that everyone desires.

Even though, liking between people may lead to loving, loving is much deeper than liking. A mother loves her physically or mentally handicapped child, but not because he is attractive. A missionary working in the remote area in an underdeveloped corner of the world loves the natives, but not because they are necessarily likable. Love is an activity of human consciousness. It is a deep concern for one's fellow being, a desire to reach out in friendship, an urge to share one's time, talents, and possessions and a willingness to accept others with their limitations and weaknesses.

Sex is one of the most significant and powerful media of love for loving couples. When couples get older, their love should not diminish because of decreased sexual activities. Sex has to be considered as one of the many media of love.

Sharing material things, accepting each other as one is, having meaningful communication, opening up the innermost feelings, fears, and dreams to one another, going out together, sharing responsibilities, and taking care of each other in sickness and in troubled times, are all expressions of love along with sex.

The overemphasis on sex and youthfulness has distorted the meaning of love in modern times. Today, a good many young people tend to go after physical appearance, talents, money, and education in choosing partners, and they de-emphasize the value of love. As a result, relationships lack the depth and growth necessary to keep them alive. Sooner or later, when the novelty wears off or when physical and material qualities diminish, the relationship dissolves. But with love, the novelty can never wear out. In a good many marriages that end up in divorce, there never was real love between the couples. It was probably physical attraction, convenience, money, power and usefulness that held them together. More than ever in our society, we have to rediscover love.

Love is a dynamic phenomenon, a growing relationship. It begins when people feel for each other, and reach out beyond physical, material, and intellectual qualities and into the spiritual. Love between a man and a woman fills their consciousness with an eagerness to give, care for, and enrich each other's personalities. The fuel for the growth of love is kindness. Giving from one partner motivates the other, and a chain of giving and taking can be established with a feeling of security and fulfillment.

The Sex Symbol

Sexual exploitation in the media and environment diminishes the human potential to give. The environmental stimuli abruptly activate emotions. If one's private environment is furnished with pornographic magazines and materials, the chances are that one will think about sex more often than in the absence of these materials. Consequently, lust will quite often dominate him. This could create in him a depersonalized sexual addiction. Psychologically, this slavery to one's passions could develop a utilitarian personality, whereby he tends to value one's physical qualities, and their usefulness. The increasing cases of rape, prostitution, venereal diseases, and illegitimate pregnancies are the outcome of this condition. The sexual anarchy and misuse increase according to the sexual stimulants in the environment.

In our licentious society, a child in elementary school, and especially in an urban environment could, due to lack of proper sex education, grow up with the misconception that sex is just an item of enjoyment, like a candy bar. If parents and teachers leave it to the students themselves, they might experiment with sex and develop emotional hang-ups with devastating consequences. On the other hand, certain children's books on the market intended to show the facts of life, can only be labeled as child pornography. They can do nothing except arouse one's sexuality. Teaching solely the sensuous aspect of sex, to children could breed a generation of sensation seekers. Sex has to be taught as one of the media of love, along with other media like sharing and caring. The physiological functions of sex, if taught well, will enable children to consider sex as a biologically important phenomenon. This could alleviate any phobias they have concerning sex and the transition to puberty, at the same time enabling them to consider sex as more than just sweet chocolate.

The Consecrated Love

If love legalized and confirmed by the institution of marriage is the only certification for having sex, how can man ignore the biological urge of concupiscence from the time of puberty to the time of matrimony? Given the way the media and environment are infiltrated with sex, it is not easy. Self-restraint is an attitude many sages have practiced. But for the secular, with a weak mind and strong body, outlets of this biological need cannot be a deadly sin. It would be easier if, by the age of puberty, an individual were educated and responsible enough to get into a stable love relationship. Judging by the acceleration with which children mature physically, emotionally, and intellectually these days, it should not be too long before the age of partnerships comes down considerably, although nuptials are delayed considerably. The stability of a marriage, regardless of age, depends on the solidarity of the values with which one lives. For maturity in marriage, value education is important.

In order to investigate the reasons behind so many marriages breaking up, we have to understand the essential nature of his institution. In the general sense, marriage could be considered as a public declaration of love between couples who are involved. In the past, however, when and where we had male-dominated societies, marriage was a declaration of ownership of a woman by a man. The wife was enslaved into the less important responsibility of maintaining affairs within the house, with very little freedom to participate in social events. There was no equality between husband and wife at any level. The brutality of the social norms in the past did not give woman any freedom of opinion, let alone the right to complain. Marriage was a relationship enforced by man on woman (still prevalent in some societies).

In Western societies, things changed fast. Education was a breakthrough for women into social freedom. Marriage became an assertion of love between couples. But later, the depth and meaning of love was washed away by the current of materialism and the sexual revolution. Selfishness, egotism, and intolerance diminished the power of love. What we need today is a revitalization of the power of love. Loving has to be much deeper than liking, even though liking usually marks the beginning of love. Certain compatibility in a couple's likes and dislikes and traits of personality often triggers love. But once love holds them together, each partner has to accept the other without resentment and try to value the other beyond physical and intellectual potentials and shortcomings. When their relationship attains the level of total involvement, anything that one does for the other should become unconditional, with no expectation of a reward of any kind. When couples take delight in such constant giving beyond reason, it can be called true love. Marriage begins only when this kind of stability and permanence is established between the couples, regardless of the matrimonial ceremony itself. Without this kind of an attachment, the matrimonial bond between couples is questionable. The essence of marriage does not lie in the piece of paper couples sign, or in the wedding gowns and the cake. It is in the contract of love between the consciousnesses of two people. If marriage could meet such spiritual standards, it would mark a decrease in the divorce rate. As it is today, many couples live in wedlock, keeping their distance, entertaining their own little dreams and demands, and waiting for criticism and finally a big letdown, divorce.

Love involves sacrifice, and for a true lover, there is a great satisfaction in it. Giving up smoking for her sake, waiting for him when he comes back from work, and staying up beside her bed when she is in the hospital are the kinds of self-fulfilling expressions of love that keep it glowing. In love, there is no selfishness, no manipulation, no dominance, and no holding back at any level. It is a total sharing, a mutual growing, a heaven for the sake of heaven.

Food is considered to be a medium for sensory enjoyment, physical health, and creative energy, all linked together. Sex has to be seen as the medium for sensual enjoyment, loving, and perpetuation of human race, all taken together. However, sex has to be considered primarily as a medium for love more than anything else. As for the conception part of sex, a bit of thinking has to be done. The birth of a child in wedlock is the precious gift of love of married couples. A child is a gift of God unlimited in value to be accepted, appreciated, and nourished by the parents. During copulation, of the millions of sperm cells that are produced, only one might make the union with the ovum. It is definitely not the intention of nature for each sperm cell to end up in conception. A sperm cell or an ovum by itself shares the spiritual energy of a man or woman. If not fertilized, they lose this energy.

Birth control, especially in our times due to the problems related to overpopulation, has become a necessary discipline we have to impose on ourselves. In many underdeveloped countries, especially in rural areas where most people are uneducated, natural methods of controlling the birth rate simply do not work. In such situations, a family struggling to stay alive with ten children should not be allowed to go on having children, thereby threatening the whole family with utter poverty and starvation. In such cases, it is a matter of conscience to educate them and make accessible artificial methods of birth control. To save a child from being born into lifelong misery is an act of concern, love, and responsibly. God has given us the intelligence and awareness to save ourselves from our limitations and weaknesses. Using artificial means of birth control solely on the basis of self-interest could be wrong, but if done out of love or concern for humanity, it would be a sanctified virtue.

The story is totally different after the union of the sperm and the egg. A zygote is a human being, to be respected as any other on earth. He or she is as much a person as the born child. Unlike the ovum, a zygote is not just a cell of the female body, even though it takes its nourishment directly from her. The zygote has an independent life that the egg or sperm cell does not have. Therefore abortion of the unborn is as serious as taking the life of a born child. The arguments by proponents of abortion, that the zygote is a part of the female body, are only as convincing as saying that the born baby is part of the female body. A zygote would not develop into a replica of its mother, but into a unique human being with a distinct personality.

The US senators who argue for providing federal funds for abortion have to realize that this would increase irresponsibility and carelessness on the part of the individuals as abortion becomes as simple an affair as a haircut. Those who argue that abortion is a privilege of the rich should argue toward complete prohibition of it, because killing is bad for both rich and poor. If anyone is worried about providing funds for accommodating unwanted babies and unwed mothers, they might soon start worrying about the waste of money on the severely handicapped and terminally sick. Prevention could be worse than cure if inhuman methods are employed.

Intelligence as the Medium of Love

Intelligence is almost always involved with matter and the senses regarding acting as a medium for living and loving. The only time when intelligence is kept out, is when one is overpowered by the intensity of his emotions. All human instincts that are triggered by one's senses can be transformed into thoughts and actions, but only with the help of the exercise of reason. Reason can either function creatively or destructively, depending on the attitudes and values formed by one's consciousness. From the invention of stone tools in the Stone Age to the inventions of the Space Age, man has been maneuvering with tools and machines for creative and destructive purposes. Creative inventions have made life easier by opening up new avenues of comfort and enjoyment. The modern means of communication, transportation, and production have saved us time and labor and given us opportunities for better living. Louis Pasteur, Alexander Graham Bell, Madame Curie, and Albert Einstein, who made life comfortable for us, will be remembered in history as great humanitarians who dedicated their lives to the well-being of men on earth.

The functions of intelligence can be classified as those for living and those for loving. When a baby is born, his brain already has the potential for intelligent behavior. In the case of a calf, as soon as he is on all fours, he knows where to find his food and starts heading toward the udders of his mother. With the human baby, however, the slower development of physical strength and coordination does not allow him to stand up. He shows signs of intelligent behavior in many other ways. The increasing complexity and mobility of our society have made it possible for little children to know a lot at an early age. To the surprise of many of us, we see six-year-olds riding bicycles and obeying traffic laws in crowded streets. The IQs of many ten-year-old's are better than those of their parents. This might be attributed to the emphasis on childhood education and the influence of social media.

Americans educate their children for a brighter future, just like anybody else in the world. Intellectual growth and accumulation of knowledge are for better living. The more technical and professional know-how one acquires, the better his chances are for comfortable living and material prosperity. Just before the energy crisis began to echo on our horizons, the old American dream of prosperity was about to materialize for almost everyone. Even today, when prosperity is a bit dimmer, many people have second cars, nice cottages, and annual vacations where the skies are always blue. Intelligence and talents have served well as the media for better living, at least in the western hemisphere. In this society, which is protected by social assistance and unemployment benefits, the problems are not so much financial as they are psychological. Divorce, violence, racism, teenage alcoholism, drug addiction, venereal diseases, juvenile prostitution, unwed motherhood, abortion, and loneliness, are all the causes of eroded morality. It is the indifference in using one's intelligence as the medium to establish interpersonal relationships, is at the root of many of these problems.

Not everyone is an Einstein. So instead of talking about using our creative geniuses for a brand-new invention with unlimited possibilities, let us talk about our own little worlds, the factories and the offices where we work. If one is concerned about others and realizes that whatever he does affects the lives of a large number of people, he should ask himself whether whatever he does serves others beneficially. This is a very difficult point to consider. The people involved in manufacturing items of basic human needs, like automobiles or pharmaceutical products, could credit themselves with using their skills for the benefit of others. Their efforts could be considered as activities of love. But what about the people who are involved in the manufacture of nuclear arms or even cigarettes? They are probably not conscious of the destructive consequences of their work. A person who is employed at an establishment that produces such goods might be a loving and concerned human being. As for the complete disarmament of nations, we are trapped in the cold war of a demoniac complex. If a good many cigarette factories were shut down or production was decreased, it could create a lot of unemployment. Then again, such an act would not prevent the employers from starting some new industries useful for man and the employees, or from finding more worthwhile jobs. But cigarette smoking is an addiction, and cigarette factories cannot be shut down. One has to look for methods to minimize the production and consumption of cigarettes through educating the public about the ill effects of smoking. As long as the shops carry cigarettes, people are going to buy them. There probably will come a time when the environment does not lend itself to developing hang-ups and weaknesses in man. That day, if it ever comes, is not in the near future.

Being smart in society today means playing games with one another, using all the tricks in the book for self-interest, power, prestige, gain, and possessions. From the waiter who smiles at you for a bigger tip to the car dealer who gives you a free cup of coffee and lots of sweet talk to close a deal, everyone is playing his own cards. There is nothing wrong with the waiter's smile and the card dealer's sweet talk, as long as the intention is fair. Also, it is humane to serve customers with respect. But in our daily lives, how often do we get taken by the Shylocks of modern times? We, the slaves of our senses and the advertising media, spend money on garbage without even realizing that we care being taken in. There is not much time to reason when someone walks into a department store and ends up buying many unnecessary items, wasting dollars. Manufactures know how to advertise their products. They associate patriotism, femininity, masculinity, and such, with their products. The average citizen, who dreams of being part of the great American heritage, or a ladies' man, or a sexy lady, ends up believing every word they say. Words like tallest, biggest, and most are dear to a typical city folk.

With mechanical extensions of our hands and legs, and computerized extensions of our brainpower, the possibility of creativity as well as destructiveness has increased. If we can transplant a heart in a matter of hours, we can also destroy the world in a matter of minutes, with nuclear weapons. We waste our brainpower and resources, trying to solve problems that we carelessly create, rather than trying to prevent them. Our medical technology is more curative than preventive. We consume great amounts of painkillers for our aches and pains, rather than get treatment for the root problems. We set up environments that lead to obesity, high blood pressure, unwanted pregnancies, venereal diseases, addiction to drugs and alcohol, and we spend time and energy fighting a losing battle against them.

Freedom does not lie in releasing our weaknesses. The problem is that in spite of all the big talk about our adulthood, we still act like spoiled children, unable to control our negative attitudes. We sit and watch our children drink poison right before our eyes, and then we run around complaining about it. Our schools have to do more than fill up children's brains with the three 'R's. If school boards could provide enough psychological help for some children to fight their negative attitudes and develop positive ones, we could save millions spent on reform schools, mental institutions, and jails.

Consciousness as the Medium of Love

As I mentioned earlier, love is more of a matter of consciousness than of intelligence or sensory experiences. For our senses and intelligence to become media for love, the consciousness has to be behind them. Just as an environment of sensory stimulants activates the desires of the sensorium or a scholastic atmosphere activates our intelligence, a spiritual environment activates our consciousness. But what could be a spiritual environment in a multicultural, multiracial, and multireligious society?

Regardless of multiplicity and diversity of any kind, freedom, love, and truth and the positive attitudes and habits should be desirable spiritual qualities to any human being.

How can we bring love and positive attitudes to a world erupting with violence and negative attitudes? In the near past, people developed their consciousness and positive attitudes through media, which emphasized the basic human values. Movies, plays, and songs talked about love and peace. People were inspired by stories and movies like Romeo and Juliet, A Tale of Two Cities, and War and Peace. Shakespeare, Dickens, and Tolstoy had something positive to offer, rather than aggravate and glorify human weaknesses and hang-ups. They proclaimed the victory of the virtues and defeat of the villainy in man. They demonized violence to the point of developing in man an aversion toward it. Books for children were filled with stories of great people who inspired them to grow up in goodness. Sports taught them cooperation, teamwork, and the ability to cope with success and defeat. There was more closeness between neighbors, more trust, more respect, and more concern. Loving was easier then, and society produced great humanitarians who were not after publicity, power, and money.

Humility, respect, kindness, cooperation, patience, responsibility, and honesty were highly honored virtues. The old media was concerned about the promotion of these attitudes, which resulted in the development of quality conscience in man. Today's media—television, movies, magazines, and the Internet—are concerned more with making a profit than promoting values. Values in modern times are whatever satisfies human senses, however dangerous the immediate or faraway consequences might be. Violence in modern media is falsified into positive value, a desirable quality. If there is plenty of violence in the environment of a growing child, this certainly is going to have an effect on his personality. A child in our society develops many of his attitudes from the behavior of his parents and especially from the shows he watches. Some time ago, in Canada, the Ontario Royal Commission on Violence in the Communication Industries, headed by Judy La Marsh, performed a two-year study and released its report in June 1977, affirming that there is a definite link between violence in the media and in society. In the United States, the National Association of Broadcasters adopted a family viewing principle in 1975, by which they established the early hours of the evening as family viewing hours. Independent stations were given an exemption until September 1, 1977, to finish off their scheduled series programs.

Children especially are easily influenced by the sensory experiences, and they tend to emulate the aggressive behavior they see in the media. If they get used to watching violence, it could develop into an addiction, a desire to watch and enjoy violence. The addiction to aggressiveness that children develop psychologically is due to continuous exposure to media violence is expressed in unprovoked vandalism and unprecedented vulgarities. In 1972–1979 in the United States, vandalism and its prevention were estimated to cost hundreds of millions of dollars. Increasing security and patrol forces would not solve the problem. The problems have their roots in the attitudes children develop through television and schools. The family is no longer a stable structure, that induces self-discipline in children. The responsibilities of schools are increasing all the more. It is estimated that in every six children under eighteen in the United States lives in a single-parent home, and most of them have working mothers. Homicides among juveniles are also increasing. The less control over guns, the more homicides there are. When some people lose their temper, their intelligence and consciousness die with it.

Violence in sports and entertainment can also induce an addiction in the viewers. Just like cigarette smoking, the more we watch violence and enjoy watching it, the more we depend on it for entertainment. Today, the more violent a show is, the larger the crowd; the rougher the game, the higher the turnout. Lots of us derive a devilish satisfaction by seeing blood in sports and in shows. As a result, we gradually develop a killer instinct, intolerance, and disrespect. We set up the environment for disaster and then try to prevent it from happening. The philosophy of modern media is to accept people as they are with all their hang-ups—and then cater to their dehumanizing cravings, inducing an addiction and making money in the process. Drug addicts will pay any price for drugs, and violence addicts will pay for violence. If bad music, bad movies, bad magazines, and marijuana cater to their needs, it is a free society for them. The promoters and producers would do anything to protect their so called "freedom."

The International Narcotics Control Board of the UN is concerned about the increased use of heroin in many countries where the drug has not been a problem before. In the early 1970s, Turkey was the major heroin supplier to the United States. Following an official complaint from the United States, the problem has been controlled using strict measures. But Mexico took over Turkey's role and supplied about 90 percent of the heroin used in thirteen major US cities in the first part of 1975.

The laws regarding the possession and use of drugs may vary in different areas of the United States. There is increased pressure to legalize certain drugs, even from some government authorities. But once the dug is legalized, moderation in use is up to the individual. The problem here is that many of us, especially children, do not know the meaning of moderation. There are millions of individuals who are prone to addiction due to lack of self-control. Drugs, including marijuana, intensify the sensory experiences and modes of behavior, and they decrease self-awareness. They can do great damage to naturally aggressive and criminal individuals. Also, there is increased danger of progression toward harder drugs in many cases. Today's 'Opioid Crisis' is unparalleled.

Under legalized distribution, the availability and acceptability would increase the use of drugs, especially among children. If there has been any decrease in the number of drug users under liberal laws, it might have been due to massive drug prevention programs or due to inaccurate data. Also, long-range effects of continuous use of drugs on the brain or on hereditary factors are not well researched.

Alcoholism is more a worldwide problem than drugs. Some of the statistics according to 1975 reports are as follows. A British report indicated that there were at least 26 million lost working days a year due to alcoholism, at the cost of £26 million to the country. Statistics from the French government showed that alcoholism killed 22,000 citizens a year. According to West German reports, an increasing number of children as young as ten were becoming alcoholics. National Institute on Alcohol Abuse and Alcoholism report in the United States showed that about one-seventh of twelfth graders get drunk at least once a week, and alcoholism was estimated to cost the country $25 million a year. In the case of drugs, restriction and imposed discipline, are inevitable due to the simple fact that society today is not that self-disciplined.

In essence, love is a fundamental theme of the life drama. This theme of love is a dynamic fulfillment amount subjects, which accomplishes fulfillment through sharing material articles and, most importantly, oneself. Sharing and communion with others gives us a feeling of well-being, a feeling of inner harmony and peace, a feeling of lasting happiness and fulfillment. Lack of love create discord among subjects and consequently causes a deviation from the evolutionary growth of personality. Love acts as an incentive for freedom, or for the development of our creative potential, as we shall see in the next chapter.

3

FREEDOM—
WHAT IS IT?

Above me was the endless light-blue sky, blown up and glazed all over by the hot bright sun. Below me was the Rockies, showing their sharp, monstrous snowbound teeth, as if to bite into our little aircraft. Clusters of clouds moved slowly, hiding at times behind the ridges like guerrilla fighters in the wilderness. Fir trees cast their shadows along the banks of a small lake they guarded, and the sun, reflecting on its crystalline icy surface, almost blinded me. Not far away, a flock of wild geese flew west and assumed different formations, as in the intermission show at a football game. I felt a sense of freedom.

But with all its serious implications, what is freedom? We cannot find unanimity among the classical definitions of freedom. According to Aristotle, man is as free at times as he is not at other times. Kant thought that pure reason, unblemished by our sensual passions, is the source of human freedom. But how pure could our reason get in a world of opposing and ambivalent ideologies? Hegel advocated that man could achieve freedom only by service to the state, and that at times he had to be forced to be free.

Fundamentally, freedom has to be achieved within individuals to have it implemented successfully in society. Epictetus was right in saying that the wicked man is never free. Milton distinguished license from liberty. The source of liberty to him was the goodness within man. Carlyle said that true liberty lies in finding the right path. But the meanings of the right path and goodness are always debatable.

For the most part, philosophical definitions have always been too subjective. A definition that we could consider as interdisciplinary, even though fundamentally philosophical, has to be both subjective and objective, and it extends to the realms of environment, individuals, and society. Out of these considerations, we could define freedom as the dynamic development of the capability for creativity, where this capability could be developed through overcoming the limitations and weaknesses in the environment, the individual, and society. Limitation could be thought of as something that we do not have or have not developed, whereas weakness is something that we learned to the wrong way. For example, not knowing how to drive is a limitation, whereas being a bad driver is a weakness. On the environmental level, the limitations are related to the restrictions of space, time, and natural resources on us. The weaknesses like diseases, pollution, and poisons are inflicted upon the environment by living organisms. In individuals, the limitations are the result of physical and psychological handicaps or the underdevelopment of our potential, whereas the weaknesses are the negative attitudes in man that express themselves in inhuman and unhealthy activities. Social weaknesses and limitations are the extensions of individual limitations and weaknesses, and they are manifested in the realms of politics, economics, religions, cultural, and racial differences.

Environmental Freedom

The Lilies of the Field

There was a time when the lilies of the field were left alone. Not anymore! Industrial chemicals and other forms of pollutants stand as the threat even to the weeds. Limitations by themselves are not bad because they motivate growth, whereas weaknesses could demolish growth. Limitations of space, time, and natural resources could be called environmental limitations. We shall go through each them.

Spatial Limitations

The moment we are born, we are limited cosmically to a particular planet, the earth, and a particular geographic area. To the early inhabitants of earth, this spatial limitation acted as a challenge in their search for food and fertile land. They invented farming so they could stay in one place, made weapons to attack animals effectively, and created clothing to keep them warm and clean. As a result of intellectual curiosity, man's horizon gradually expanded, and his world increased in complexity. All scientific discoveries down through the centuries increased human interaction on the globe.

The world shrunk as a result of mass media and communication. Transportation on land and in air translated miles into minutes. The one-time mysteries of heavenly bodies became objects of scientific interests. It was necessity, that mothered all the great inventions, and shortened the distance between continents, cultures, and even between celestial bodies.

Limitations of Time

Time and space limitations are closely related factors, and overcoming any one of these would lead to overcoming the others. What took days and months for prehistoric man can be done today in a matter of minutes or hours. For primitive men, finding and cooking food were full-time jobs. Today, we have better things to do with our time. The world of machines has freed man from being tied up by any job, and it has given him enough time to read, relax, and entertain himself. Time is increasingly gaining momentum with newer inventions. As a result, we should be able to increase more and more the quality and quantity of our activities. Scientific technology has narrowed the gap between past and present, and the present and future.

The human psyche has unlimited potential, which could one day take man into times and places at an instant. Talk about time machines should be considered as much more than mere myth.

Shortage of Natural Resources

The Neanderthal men who fished, hunted, and plucked fruits from trees had to go from place to place in search of new natural resources. Men of the Paleolithic, Mesolithic, and Neolithic Ages had plenty of everything. Until recent times, the inhabitants of the earth never felt a shortage of natural resources. Men lived on this planet for centuries like born millionaires, without ever realizing that there would come a time of shortage. Mother Earth nourished us well, giving everything she had. Now that she is worn out, we as adults who can no longer be too dependent on her resources, have to look to the nuclear and solar energies for survival.

When coal was replaced by oil as a cleaner and cheaper source of energy, nobody took time to think that a shortage of it would come someday. The latest surveys show that the oil shortage is almost an emergency. There are, of course, scientist who dispute this with the argument that the earth could give us oil for hundreds of years. It would be unintelligent to wait until its gone, to do something about it. The conversion of coal into clean fuel, tapping the solar and nuclear energy sources, etc., were timely recommendations to the Congress by former President Carter, but they should take time to achieve substantial productivity. It is unwise to not get on with these projects, until oil becomes a rare and priceless commodity like some costly cologne. The initial expenses for building solar energy platforms in space would be great, but it should be considered as inevitable procedures, if man is to cope with the speed with which other energy resources are running out.

All human needs are basically dependent on energy resources, in a world of technology and overpopulation. In countries with the highest population growth and lowest income, the demand for food is becoming severe. The agricultural revolution, referred to universally as the Green Revolution was launched in the 1970s to cope with this demand. High-yielding varieties of plants, irrigation, fertilizers, pesticides, and herbicides, require great energy inputs. Refining and distributing food also requires energy. Climatic changes pose a great problem to cultivation. The devastating drought in the African Shabel belt a few years ago, where rainfall had been rare for six years, is considered to be the result of a southward shift in wind patterns. Unexpected climatic changes have paralyzed food production at times in North America in recent years. There is a no definite proof as to the effect of sunspot changes on the earth's climate.

The great demand for the cereals like wheat, rice, and corn to feed large populations force us to look for new substitutes. Oil seeds are a great source of protein. Potentially eighty million tons of protein-rich oil seeds are available per year for human consumption, after the extraction of oil. The main bulk of it is either discarded or used as animal feed or fertilizer. However, it requires additional refining to be used by man.

Many of our problems today are the result of mismanagement of energy resources. We need more humanistic planning of energy usage. In technological energy consumption, priority has to be given to fundamental human needs like clean air, good eating, good health care, shelter, clothes, education, communication, transportation, and new resources of energy. Unfortunately, in highly technological societies, enormous quantities of energy and fuel are being used for entertainment and luxuries without first adequately taking care of the basic human needs. Means of transportation and communication should come before alcoholic beverages, toys, or entertainment. Economically speaking, shipping extra food to underdeveloped counties may not be worth it. But for humanitarian reasons, every penny spent on it is a token of love. The world largely depends on the United States for food, and US agriculture consumes large quantities of fuel. This is one of the most humanitarian ways by which energy is being used in the United States.

Poison Ivy

Overcoming the limitations and developing our potential would be a fascinating experience, if nature did not stand in the way of our progress. Natural weaknesses like catastrophes, pollution, and diseases can at times overpower us in our struggle to free ourselves. It would be interesting to dig into the roots of the "poison ivy" of the environment.

Matter was good as it was created. Poisonous substances like potassium cyanide or carbon monoxide never existed so freely as to directly interfere with the life forms that were to appear on earth in the course of time. The micro-organisms germinating on earth were designed to preserve the balance of nature. At one time, the ecological interdependence of soil, plants, and animals was creative and comforting to all parties involved.

If we accept the accusation that man is the only troublemaker, how can we account for the fact that there were disease-spreading germs and poisonous plants even before man showed his face on earth? The forces of good and evil fought each other—one trying to sustain life, the other trying to destroy freedom. If certain bacteria could help the digestive systems of higher life forms, there were viruses that could inflict deadly diseases upon them. The same was the case in the plant kingdom. There were plants supporting and sustaining creation as a source of food, oxygen, and aesthetics, and there were plants producing poisonous vegetation. How could there be a paradox?

This question cannot be explained adequately without understanding the phenomenon of life itself. The mystery of the formation of life from nonliving molecules has not been explained scientifically. Understanding the chemistry within galaxies, according to some scientist, would lead to possible answers. To the theist, the amazingly brilliant ways by which the universe is designed and developed and the implantation of life in molecules are the works of an omnipotent personality called God. To the atheist, everything was accidental. Man's brain, even with the help of microscopes, telescopes, test tubes, and computers, is not equipped enough to prove that the universe is either directed or accidental, but circumstantial evidence strongly suggests that the benefit of doubt has to be given to the theist's stand, to the fact that complexity of the universe and of life had to be designed by a Super Brain.

Let us briefly examine some of the scientific theories on the origin of life. The composition of life is determined to be an average of that of the universe and the earth. It has been suggested that, life arose on earth, when the chemical composition of the earth was much closer to the cosmic composition, before the earth's composition might have changed, somehow. Ninety-nine percent of the universe and life is made of six atoms each, of hydrogen, helium, carbon, nitrogen, oxygen, and neon.

As the story goes, it started in the sea. The sea was like a warm bowl of soup of organic molecules. The atoms had been joining together to form molecules, and molecules were getting more and more complex to produce polynucleotides with or without the help of enzymes. Then when the time was right and the environment was suitable, polynucleotides energized to produce primordial organisms. It is believed to have happened only once, and perhaps once was enough to launch a whole new history for Mother Earth. It was like a plane receiving a pilot, but it is not that simple to explain. An unsolved mystery is the origin of the genetic code that is considered to be the essence of life. As far as we know, the first functional relationship between the polynucleotides and proteins to produce the code is beyond the known molecular mechanisms. It would be a rational speculation that the code could have been the result of the incarnations of spiritual units into these complex molecules, thus producing life on earth. But I believe that these organic molecules had to attain a certain level of complexity before receiving the "spiritual waves," just as a radio has to have certain electronic complexity before receiving the radio waves. Life, by biological definition, is a "mutable and self-replicating molecular system which is able to interact with the environment." The great complexity involved in this definition could be accounted for, only if we attribute it to the spiritual units that could be thought to have inhabited these molecular systems.

If life was indeed the creation of God, then where did it go so wrong as to produce killer germs and poisonous fruits? In the history of our planet, only once did the vitalization of molecules take place. After that first appearance of living cells, evolution should have brought forth new species on earth. There are reasons to believe that evolution was brought to a halt for each species as soon as it brought forth a new species. As Georges Cuvier, the French naturalist noted, five-thousand-year-old mummified animals found by Napoleon's expedition to the Egyptian pyramids were identical with existing forms. However, he made one important observation. In rock strata of the Paris Basin, the fossils found in upper beds were relatively more complex than the ones in the lower beds. This could be taken to suggest that during the process evolution, each species went through, there were gradual changes in complexity until a new species emerged. As soon as that happened, the preceding species stopped evolving. If the evolution was a continuous process, all the unicellular organism would have had evolved into higher forms by now. On the other hand, it can be supposed that each species evolved into a new one and then stopped suddenly. This brilliant setup again could be attributed to a master mind, who established an efficient ecological system. We need plants to support animal and human life. If they evolved into something else, it would have been difficult for the animals and men who depend so much on the plants for their existence.

Creation of Evolution?

When Charles Darwin released his theory of evolution, biblical theologians scratched their heads and tried to label it as a heresy. The problem was that many of them considered the accounts of creation contained in Genesis as literally true, unaware of the fact that they were written by prophets who were a select. The message that the biblical accounts of creation may convey, could be that God created units of life and co- directed the evolution with the living organisms. There doesn't have to be a contradiction between creation and evolution. In fact, if there is a contradiction, both the theory of creation and the theory of evolution would remain incomplete with many unanswered questions. Even before Charles Darwin, people like Montesquieu, and Charles Darwin's grandfather Erasmus Darwin had suggestions about the possibility of evolution. It was Charles who systematically organized the mechanism of evolution. Genetics and paleontology later supported and supplemented the theory to be authentic, although several questions still remain.

The process of evolution of the species is thought to be the result of mutation in a sperm cell or an egg cell. A mutation is considered a mistake of the gene in copying itself, thus altering the physical and psychic replication of the organism in the offspring.

Many inherited mutations can cause harmful diseases such as hemophilia, muscular dystrophy, and albinism. Lethal mutations could cause complete handicaps in an offspring. But there are mutations that will create an offspring better adaptable to the changing environment, and thus better able to survive in the process of natural selection. It is believed that the mutation and natural selection control the process of evolution. But what we do not know is why only at particular time periods such massive mutations occurred to bring about a new species. If mutation was accidental, such organized hierarchy of species without close intermediate links between them is beyond reason. It has to be argued that the mutations that mark the beginning of a new species are directed. Otherwise, why did such evolutionary mutations take place only once for each species?

What, then, could be the key to the evolutionary momentum? This question can be answered only if a proper distinction is made between human and subhuman behavior. An animal today behaves more or less the same way as his ancestors did ten thousand years ago. But not man. Man is capable of improving his activities. A spider's web hasn't changed considerably with time or environment. The design is almost the same, whether it is eons ago or today, in the city or in the jungle. The story of man is not so. Regardless of time and place, he has continuously and consciously improved on his habitats. He has taken command of the environment and changed it to suit his acting needs. Animals can only adjust or adapt to the changing environment; they cannot change the environment itself. Every subhuman species has a limit to which it can develop its brain power on its own. And they do not seem to experiment beyond these limits. That may be why the spider's web is about the same anywhere and at any time, or why intelligent animals like the dolphin are not much more creative or inventive than their ancestors. Any new behavior, which is self-motivated rather than merely conditioned or adapted, has to be learned with a great degree of self-conscious effort. People, especially little children, could be conditioned to behave in a particular way, just as some of the intelligent animals can be. This involves limited mental processes because there is no self-determination or critical evaluation. The self-awareness is activated when one begins to ask why.

The incapability of animals to improve their modes of behavior and creativity from internal persuasion, is perhaps due to the limited activity of their conscious psyche. However, the first spiders to invent the web and the first bees to construct the comb must have had the gift of consciousness in order to be creative without being conditioned to do so. But the cessation of improvement on their systems, and the fact that a new, higher species had to carry the evolutionary relay beyond their current level, must be due to a fixation on this self-awareness at a limited level, which in effect contributed to ecological systemization. As a result, each species below man remained at a certain level of creativity, presumably because of divine intervention.

It is coded within the seed of a plant how tall it will grow or what shape the leaves will take. Some alteration may occur due to environmental factors. It is coded in the genes of any organism or species the various dimension of its development and behavior with slight variations, depending on the milieu. But man has the ability to develop beyond his genetic code, and to even alter the code. In this respect, man's potential for freedom is limitless. He could break the boundary. He is like a spaceship with enough power to get beyond the gravitational pull of the earth. Once there, the journey is effortless. One day, I believe, man will be there. He has the fuel for it, in terms of psychological resources.

Skinner and Pavlov could perhaps condition all animals of the same breed with prediction. Man with his unique gift of a self-conscious psyche cannot be conditioned the same way. All of us would react in our own ways to the environmental stimuli. However, it has to be noted that the less self-conscious one is, the greater would be the effect of conditioning on him. For that reason, children could be conditioned more easily than adults. With adults, everyone is not capable of self-determination to the same degree. But self-awareness could be developed by all men to any degree with effort.

This is where man differs from animals. Animals can know only the what and how, but man knows the why. In this connection, reward and punishment have to be considered as motivational factors for the what and the how rather than the factors of self-determination. Animals' awareness of the environment, self, and others is limited.

At least, during the evolutionary stages, if the micro-organisms had the power of self-determination to be creative or destructive, it is quite rational to assume that most of them used it for creativity, whereas the others used it for destructivity and deformation. The result was the beginning of diseases. The fall of angels referred to in the Bible could be this distortion, either on a purely spiritual level or on the level of micro-organisms, as weapons of eternal destructivity.

Many of the deadly diseases are inflicted by biotic agents like viruses, rickettsia, bacteria, fungi, and parasites. But not all of these organisms are dangerous. Some of them are able to survive in soil, water, or lower animals without posing any threat. As a matter of fact, a good many of them contribute creatively to the ecological setup by decomposing organic materials and returning them to the soil, and many others assist the metabolic mechanisms of higher forms of life. Then there are the "demon seeds," ready to destroy the body of the host. Viruses, which are nucleic acids enclosed in protein are among the deadliest organisms of all. Statistics show that in 1975 in the United States alone, there were close to 665,000 new cancer patients to add to the more than one million previous victims. It is assumed that one in every four living persons eventually will have cancer. It costs between $15–25 billion annually to combat this disease. Bacterial afflictions such as various types of infections and venereal diseases are much less devastating.

Modern techniques in medical science have reduced the fatality rate by better prevention or treatment of diseases. In the 1900s, cancer was always fatal. By 1930, one-fifth of all cancer patients were able to recover; and by 1975 it was one-third. Longevity had increased all over the world because of better medical care. The major factors of susceptibility today are age, nutrition, and exercise. A child at birth possesses enough antibodies to defend himself for a few months. When the antibodies are lost, there is a period of vulnerability until the infant develops new defense mechanisms. Inoculations have helped in preventing many childhood diseases, especially in underdeveloped countries, where infant mortality is usually high. Lack of proper nutrition, increases the danger of invasion by disease germs, especially in children and senior citizens. More emphasis has yet to be placed on research in preventive medicine so that we can save much money and human suffering.

Disease organisms, if considered as the deviation from the creative evolution of life, may take the blame upon themselves, for bringing so much suffering upon the human race. As I have mentioned, if all micro-organisms had the power of self-determination during the process of their evolution, it is quite rational to assume that some of them happily accepted their creative roles while others rebelled and became weapons of eternal destruction. In the same way, it might have been a deep-rooted hatred that eventually resulted in the evolution of poison glands in certain reptiles. Poisonous fruits and vegetation might have had a similar origin.

The Epidemiology of Evil

With respect to organismic evil, one could believe that because each new species might have lost its self-determining power to a new species taking over the evolutionary thrust, with man breaking into the scene, the rest of the species got fixed at various levels of structural and psychic limitations and weaknesses. Thus, we have the viruses and bacteria of epidemics and terminal diseases, the micro-organisms of metabolic activities, and the plants and animals that are creative or destructive to varying degrees, all stabilized on their own levels without any hope of evolution. Here, we have to bear in mind that most of the plant species support life all the way.

The origin of evil in the creation through micro-organisms, "the fall of the angels" who were supposed to serve the creation, could thus be initially considered as a self-determined act on the part of some primordial organisms. With evolution and inheritance, these evil tendencies might have developed in higher forms of life as well. The "forbidden fruit" and the "serpent" that tempted Eve in the Garden of Eden could thus be symbolic of this distortion in plant and animal existence; it was there before man, and it eventually influenced him.

Predetermination or Self-determination?

There have been many arguments in the past on this topic. Predetermination, based on many behavioral theories, excludes the possibility of self-determination and therefore the ability to direct one's own evolution. The pattern of growth and behavior of any non-evolving organism could be considered largely predetermined by genetic and environmental factors. In the case of a plant, on the basis of the quality of the seed and the environmental factors, its growth pattern could be predicted with a fair amount of accuracy.

Animal behavior could be predicted on the basis of genetic and environmental information, although with less accuracy. In the case of man, genetic factors and cerebral and physical structures, along with the environment, would determine the formation of his personality. But deviations from any prediction would always be possible based on the degree of development, or of the power of, self-determination in each individual. The predicable part of human behavior would also depend on his genetic endowments, tradition and habitats, as well as cultural, social, and economic backgrounds. The fact that one is born into this world, in a certain level, would predetermine a lot of things about him. But unlike other organisms, man is capable of enriching his behavior, disregarding the external influences. Whether or not one exercises his power is up to each individual. Thus, the driving factors of human evolution could be both pre-determination and self-determination. The more self-determined one is, the better his chances to develop his personality.

Individual Freedom

Free as a Bird

"I am free; I can do anything I want!" Is there such a permanent feeling? Of course we all would agree that there are many moments of freedom in our lives, the moments and days we hoped would never end. More often we tend to complain about external pressures and our inability to cope with these pressures of life. We struggle through our lives, constantly trying to free ourselves from the clutches of various systems and institutions. Our whole history is a struggle toward freedom: political, social, economic, religious, racial, and you name it.

The starting point of human freedom has to be the person himself. If man can achieve freedom within himself, he can transform it into the society and the environment of which he is a part. Before we deal with the aspect of individual freedom, it would be helpful to look at the structure of the human brain and its functions.

Man Is a Machine

Neurologists are able to compartmentalize the brain into different parts, each controlling a definite activity, by removing different parts of the brains of animals and observing the effects. Another method is to observe the changes in the behavior of people whose brains are partially damaged. During brain surgery, surgeons are able to stimulate various activities of the brain by applying a weak electrical current to various parts of the brain. They have found that when wires are placed on parts of the temporal lobe, the patient experienced memories of the past.

Categorizing the human psyche into body, mind, and spirit, on the basis of the traditional concept of the psyche is an efficient method for us to understand ourselves. No matter how many departments into which the human psyche might be classified according to psychological findings, they would all fall into one or the other above category. At least such a system would enable us to systematically study ourselves. A Trinitarian concept of human psyche bears great resemblance to the trinity in an atom, where the three atomic particles form a whole. The Trinitarian concept of the atom should also be taken as a simplification of the more complex findings.

Do You See What I See?

To talk about the evolution of the three faculties of the psyche—namely, body, mind and spirit—we have to start from the time of corpusculisation From the unicellular organisms to Homo Sapiens, there has been a gradual evolutionary development of the sensory mechanisms, with increasing complexity. With higher levels of consciousness, creatures have been able to derive more and more emotional experiences from the environment. It is not how far ones sees, but how deeply one experiences the vision, that measures the depth of a visual experience. Beauty is in the eye of the beholder.

Take, for example, the pen that I have used to write this. Ordinarily, the beauty of a pen goes unnoticed. It has a light yellow stem with a golden tip and black cap. As I look closer, I can see the contrast of the colors, the smooth look, and the geometrical shape of the pen. Any other sensory experience could become deeper in the same way with concentration. No two people can perceive beauty the same way. There are people who are born with, or have developed through childhood years, an esthetic outlook. To them, everything looks so beautiful. It is possible to develop such an attitude through conscious effort. To find beauty, one has to look for it. Nature provides us with plenty of sources, and if they are not enough, man can create more. From prehistoric times to modern times, he has been creating beauty.

With urbanization, we have lost a lot of our appetite for natural beauty. Technological man might find plastic flowers more attractive than real ones, blooming with life. The roses in his own garden perhaps don't smell nice anymore. He has to have a vacation in the Bahamas to have any esthetic experience! It is time that we looked at our own skies on a starry night and sit in our backyards enjoying the beauty, until our minds are filled with joy.

A Prick of Conscience

Intelligence is a faculty that we have developed out of necessity. The need for survival made man invent things essential for existence. The Industrial Revolution taught us to believe that happiness is hard work and making money is what life is all about. To the man of materialistic philosophy, money is power, freedom, and happiness. There is nothing much that money can't buy, even love!

The distortion of evolution in intellectual and sensational categories was due to the malformation of human consciousness through the centuries. Primitive man feared and worshipped the forces of nature that either frightened him or helped him earn a living. Thus, thunder and lightning, sun and moon, fire and water, and even snakes and cows became gods to him. When men started living together in tribal units, a code of ethics gradually emerged for the smooth interaction of its members. The laws multiplied with the increase in his activities. A sense of morality emerged in him, and consciousness began to develop.

More than anything else, it was a fear of consequences. From the ideas of gods, who were the personifications of natural powers, the idea of one god emerged, who became the creator, the sustainer of life, and the final judge. The development of religious philosophy was carried out by a minority that was able to reflect on life and its meaning, and the others followed their teachings without questioning.

With the coming of Christ, all the laws were unified in one ultimate and fundamental law—the law of love. Later, individuals and institutions monopolized the interpretation of the law of love to suit the time and people at different periods. There was a valid reason for this. The average citizen was not educated enough to apply the law of love to the specific moral dilemmas that confronted him in society. Society was like a group of small children who lacked the intellectual and moral powers to make any major decisions.

The Renaissance marked a state of adolescence for society, during which individuals questioned the prevailing state of affairs. The Reformation was one result. Calvin and Luther tried to update Christianity, and as a result Protestant churches emerged. The Catholic Church underwent great transformation and produced some of the greatest humanitarians in world history. Later, secularization began to reduce church attendance, and the word God gradually disappeared from the vocabulary of urban man. He began to replace God with money, essence with existence. The result was a breakdown in the value system. In our times, we could witness a revival of Christianity, with an emphasis on the essence beyond denominational differences.

Whatever might be the case, religion has played a tremendous role in developing human consciousness, and in my estimation, a religious revival is the only means for the continuation of this process. Those who accuse religion of being responsible for a lot of violence have to realize that it was distorted conscience of certain individuals that brought violence into religion, as they did in other social institutions. If the Old Testament prophets advocated an attitude of retaliation against the enemies, it was due to their underdeveloped consciousness, which was the sign of their times. But when Christ came, he pointed out the inadequacy of the old laws and stressed the importance of loving the enemy. Later, the old laws at times overpowered the new law of Christ, drawing blood over the question of righteousness and religious freedom.

Who Doesn't Have a Handicap?

Man can achieve freedom only if three faculties of the psyche are developed and active. But there are cases where one is born with physical or psychological handicaps, whereby he is unable to exercise to his own satisfaction one or more of these faculties, thus being enslaved by the restrictions of his physical structure.

All the human limitations could be considered as being fundamentally structural. This is true for any other creature. If the human psyche were to enter the body of a mule, it would behave like mule, because the cerebral and physical structure of the mule would not allow it to behave otherwise. Consciousness would be minimized because the development of that part of the brain that activates the consciousness would be minimal. This is to say, there is equality among the psyche of all organisms, and the differences in intelligence, sensory experiences, and consciousness are all structural. In the case of man, an intelligent, healthy, and talented human being could change its personality overnight as a result of an accident involving the damage of his brain.

We differentiate people according to the degree of development of the three faculties of the psyche and their interactions. Personality differences are the result of the differences in the structure and associations, of the nerve cells in the central nervous system, and of the coordination among the various parts of the body. Behavioral psychologists might say that man behaves according to environmental conditioning. But it is important to bear in mind the fact that in the development of the brain, not only man's environment, but also his self-determination play important roles. In other words, man has the power and potential to manipulate the growth of his intelligence and the function of his sensorium and hence his personality, according to the degree of stimulation of his consciousness. This could be done effectively during the childhood years, which are the formative years of human personality. That is why great care has to be taken in planning a curriculum for children.

The case of consciousness is entirely different from that of intelligence and sensory experiences, in that regardless of intellectual and sensory growth, a good consciousness can be developed even by the mentally handicapped. However, it is true that the depth of the consciousness is dependent on the sensory and intellectual growth as well.

Now, let us talk about the structural limitations that have to be overcome to experience freedom. Everyone is unique in physical endowments. Even through, many of us would like to be tall, strong, and well coordinated, how we will develop physically is coded into our genes. The pattern can be altered with effort, to some degree. If freedom lies in the capability for creativity, the physically handicapped are limited in executing their initiatives. Electronic equipment and advances in medical science have contributed tremendously in overcoming physical handicaps. It should not be too long before the crippled will be able to walk normally, the deaf will be able to hear, and the blind will be able to see, with surgery and electronic aids rather than a transplant. Overcoming these limitations will open up new avenues and extend the horizons of creativity for the physically handicapped.

Functional handicaps, often known as mental handicaps, are due to impaired function of the nervous system. These limitations, which close in the boundaries of creativity for the handicapped, will one day be rectified with scientific technology. Advances in genetics definitely point towards that direction. A successful attempt to prevent mental retardation by treating the fetus was described in a 1975 issue of the New England Journal of Medicine by Mary G. Ampole of the Tufts New England Medical Centre. The disorder, which involves failure to convert vitamin B12 to a useful form, results in an accumulation of acid on the fetus's body tissue, which impairs the intellect and ultimately leads to the child's death. To prevent this, the mother was administered massive doses of B12, which entered the fetal circulation.

Education of the mentally handicapped is undergoing tremendous changes. The advocates of mainstreaming believe that handicapped children could benefit from learning in regular classrooms. However, special supplementary programs are thought to be necessary. From the social standpoint, exposure to regular classroom environments, would prove to be educational for the mentally handicapped. Experts in this field from twenty-eight nations gathered in Canterbury, England, in August 1975 to discuss the problems of the handicapped. They emphasized the need for teaching the handicapped in stimulating environments. They also pointed out that the real numbers of handicapped children are underestimated.

Another form of individual limitation is man's inability to foresee the adverse consequences of industrialization. Many studies show that asbestos workers risk developing lung cancer. Inhalation of the chemical vinyl chloride monomer has proven to be the cause of angiosarcoma, a rare form of liver cancer. Tests by the FDA in the United States, as well as experiments done in Canada, reveal shocking information about the toxicity of many commonly used food products. Thus, sensory, intellectual, and awareness limitations could handicap our activities. Basically, all these limitations are structural in that they are the structural limitations of the nervous system and the physique, which minimize the psychic functions. Freedom lies in overcoming our limitations to extend the realm of human creativity. But it is not the limitations that threaten our freedom as much as human weaknesses, as we shall see.

Man the Wicked

Accidents can be the result of our limitations or weaknesses, depending on the situation. The oil spills we talk about so much lately are in many cases not a reflection of man's indifferent attitudes. It is more of a limitation of man, a lack of intellectual ability, to foresee such accidents. The explosion of an inhabited spaceship would not be premeditated. But indifferent attitudes definitely have caused a few air crashes and train collisions that claimed hundreds of human lives. Certain insecticides sprayed on farmlands and forests are reported to have crippled children and cattle in the area. These might have been unexpected events, but it is indeed indifferent and negative attitudes that have caused asbestosis in many factory workers, even after the discovery of a connection between cancer and chemicals generated in these factories.

Meteorologists and other scientists fear that man-made changes in the atmosphere and on earth could cause severe damage to the environment. Thus, smoke, combustion gases, insecticides, herbicides, industrial wastes, and aerosol sprays could induce problems in the air, land, and water environments.

Dumping of industrial wastes into the waters is another serious problem. There have been incidents of mercury poisoning in many countries because of fish from waters contaminated by mercury being eaten. To protect the waters from radiation hazards, security measures in radioactive waste disposal were announced by the OECD in May 1975. They decided to carry out an internationally supervised disposal of packaged, solid, radioactive wastes into the deep Atlantic. Even though international laws forbid dumping wastes from oil tankers within fifty miles of the coastlines, there have been violations.

Nuclear technology could be considered as the genetics of matter with enormously useful possibilities. The destructive power of nuclear weapons is enough to level the earth. The radiation from nuclear tests conducted by certain countries could have immediate or forthcoming adverse consequences on the earth's environment. As far as cigarette smokers are concerned, the warning about smoking as being dangerous to health is only a paper tiger. Attitudes and habits become addictive after a point. Once one reaches that point, consequences do not scare him.

Pollution, waste, and annihilation of wildlife without justifiable reasons have bent our environment out of shape, and we are incapable of maintaining the ecosystem. We must learn to correct our bad habits before the environment becomes too unhealthy. Fortunately, people are becoming more aware of the problems and are beginning to think seriously about their environment.

These are the weaknesses that have slowed down our material progress, because much of our energy was channeled toward fighting these evils rather than toward overcoming our limitations and developing our potential. The fight against diseases, pollution, and deadly weapons will not be successful until man can straighten out himself by eliminating his negative attitudes.

No matter how far we go in developing the powers of the intelligence and the depth of our sensory experiences, they need not necessarily promote creativity. Here is where we have to deal with our many weaknesses. The breakdown of values in modern times has resulted in the revival of the Epicurean philosophy. Our mass media directly or indirectly proclaims that the purpose of life is accumulation of material wealth and acquisition of physical comforts. This kind of attitude has broken the moral fiber of our society to the point of creating in man a vending-machine mentality. If Herbert Spencer's theory of the survival of the fittest holds true today, the fittest are the most selfish people in our society. Nice guys get run over or thrown to the sidelines.

Irresponsibility, indifference, dishonesty, disrespect, jealousy, greed, insensitivity, selfishness, and even alcoholism and drug addiction could be regarded as individual weakness and therefore hurdles to the human capacity for creativity. Major crimes are the result of man's negative attitudes. There is no way of reducing the crimes without eradicating these attitudes within individuals. This could be called the process of developing a positive conscience of consciousness.

Heaven Is Like a Mustard Seed

Because environmental and social freedoms are the extensions of the freedom within, the secret of happiness is the balance of all the three psychic faculties within man. But it is not easy to teach an old dog new tricks. Repairing or altering the malformed psyche of an adult is not easy, or at least not as easy as working with children.

Even though hereditary factors predetermine a lot of the physical and psychological growth patterns of a child, the environment manipulates the personality of a growing child to a great extent. In the case of a germinating seed, regardless of the condition of the sprout, its growth can be controlled by environmental factors.

Similarly, with children the physical and psychic growth can be controlled and directed with appropriate exercise. When a child is ready for physical activities, it would be beneficial to organize a program of exercise that develops strength and physical coordination yet suits the fragile state of his body, as is done in many nursery schools. This, together with proper nutrition, would maintain the psychical healthy of the child. Nutrition is an important factor for health not only during childhood, but throughout life. Priorities of taste and cravings for certain foods are established in man from his childhood as a habit. If a child is raised on too much sugar, he will develop an addiction to it, and everything has to taste sweet in order to be palatable. Too many candy bars and too much pop could have harmful repercussions when people grow up Diabetes and high blood pressure are some of them. It is easy to develop a taste in children for natural nutrients like fruits, vegetables, and milk, which will stay with them even when they grow up.

The depth of sensory experiences should be enhanced by a series of exercise. Most of the beauty around us often goes unnoticed. If we could create in children an esthetic awareness, that would melt into their personalities, when they grow older. In a classroom where there are a good many beautiful objects to choose from, children could be asked to pick any one object and observe it closely and in detail. The color, shape, and details in pattern, which they never noticed so closely before, might fascinate them. This exercise, if continued over a period of time, would develop in them a natural tendency to appreciate the beauty of their surroundings. It would enable them to transfer this sense into whatever they see. Such awareness is just like having a garden around the house!

Auditory experience can be enhanced in the same way. Children could be asked to close their eyes and listen to the sounds around them, with a readiness to pick up any trace of sound coming from all four directions. This exercise could be followed by asking them to listen to a recording of a soft melody with maximum concentration, getting absorbed in the vibrations of the musical notes.

The senses of smell, touch, and taste could be enhanced using flowers, warm or cold substances, and food. Exercises like those would invigorate sensory awareness, and the child could develop a pleasant self. As for the intellectual faculty, the methods and media of instruction have made tremendous headway in recent years. The self-research techniques widely employed in schools today have increased the originality of thought in children.

Children should be encouraged to peruse their intellectual curiosity with an attitude of "Why?" rather than "Why not?", which presupposes a conclusion and demands justification rather than an open-minded search.

The development of consciousness in children could be done using a variety of methods. To the adherents of child-centered ideology, which are paramount today, include the Latin term enducere, which means "to lead out." In subject-centered ideology, the term means "to bring up." When it comes to value education, we have to deal with each child according to his emotional growth. Children are prone to be manipulated by the environment, or what goes into their heads, through their senses. Consciousness is underdeveloped in them. The environment outside the classroom, especially in city streets and broken homes, can only weaken their consciousness or conscience. Setting up a classroom with all kinds of tools for creativity need not always promote creativity in every child, especially in the ones who have already developed negative aptitudes. The teacher's responsibility is to bring out the good and cast out the bad, as well as to educate children about how their actions affect the environment, the self, and others.

Many of the habits formed in early childhood years stay with people even when they grow up. In old times, parents and teachers used to place greater significance on teaching the children etiquette and manners. Words and phrases like "please," "may I," and "thank you" are gradually disappearing from the vocabulary of children, and words of command, conditions, and swearing are replacing them. Respect for others is something that has to be taught from early childhood. Giving respect is a precondition for earning respect.

Experiments done in Europe and America on environment and behavior in preschool children indicate that good and bad behavior patterns form as early as ages one and two, depending on the environment. Toys can be a determining factor in developing attitudes in children. Many toys like yo-yos, kites, and baby dolls are beneficial for little minds, but guns, war machines, and stunt figures could cultivate undesirable interests in them. Dolls especially would have an idolizing effect on the innocent minds. According to the 1975 US toy sales records, about 11 percent of sales were of dolls. Toys and games for children should be designed to promote creative attitudes, thus enriching the benefits of education.

The curriculum content of childhood education is also gradually getting away from its devotion to fundamental values. It may be filled with inspiring stories about great people. The stories were intended to develop in children an affinity toward virtues like honesty, cooperation, kindness, hard work, patience, respect, and the like. Many a child in the past has changed his habit of telling lies after being inspired by the story of George Washington and his honesty. Today, many stories are either fabricated or merely entertaining. Attitudes like sharing or caring could be taught through their application in classroom situations. It is easy and important to establish good habits and positive attitudes before children get into the grade six level. Usually, children begin to lose the touch of innocence toward the end of grade six, with a great shift in their attitudes. Children who have been enthusiastic until then, about helping the teacher to carry classroom responsibilities, like cleaning, could become increasingly reluctant, even to clean their own mess, except for a few volunteers who were brought up by their parents to be that way. The important thing about developing habits and attitudes in children is that, they should never be forced to behave for fear of consequences. It should be the result, more of inspiration than enforcement. But with some children, enforcement would be the only way of initiation.

Disciplining children, from grades seven and up is becoming increasingly challenging for teachers. If a child does not get any discipline at home, it is of no use how much discipline the teacher gives him. In many cases, the teacher is wasting his time fighting with a parent who says, "My kid is okay." Some parents fail to realize that the personality of a child can change from one grade to another, depending on the environment and on physical and psychological changes. Some children might behave well at home and be entirely the opposite in the midst of their peers. Year after year, the teacher's job is getting more and more difficult. They probably need those two months off in the summer to get ready for the next school year, by taking lessons in defense mechanisms like karate and transcendental meditation!

Reasoning and love, and at times firm persuasion, are the only effective correctional methods that could produce any result in some of the more aggressive children.

The what, the how and the why!

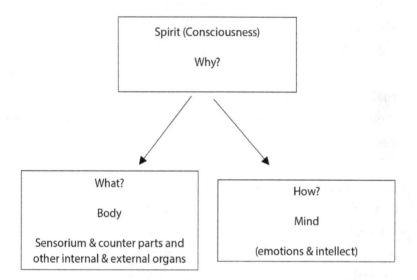

The five human senses are always curious about the what of things. They concentrate mainly on identifying and appreciating the external details of objects. Intelligence is anxious to analyze an object and find out how it is constituted. Intellectual discoveries enable us to see the basic principles for newer inventions. Why is a quest of the consciousness or conscience, and involves value judgements.

Emotions develop in man directly due to the function of his sense. As a result, he tends to respond immediately to an environmental stimulus. However, his feelings should not be let loose to take complete possession of him, because when this happens, his intelligence may invent ways to satisfy his needs, sometimes failing to judge the value of the methods being used. If his consciousness or conscience is strongly formed, he tends to evaluate his needs and ask himself for moral justification, for his actions. But when passions get strong, the consciousness sometimes fails to function. This results at times in adopting unconventional methods to meet the needs. This slavery within oneself could injure society, thus jeopardizing social freedom. Man often tries to justify his weaknesses with reason. Rationality, dominated by ones' passions and selfishness, is actually irrationality. Such irrationality or negative rationality is due to the underdevelopment of one's consciousness or conscience.

As I emphasized before, loose connections among the three psychic faculties can create problems. Sensory experiences and intelligence, if not coordinated, could create in man poor reflexes, absentmindedness, oversensitivity, emotional outbreaks, and more. Intellectual control is most essential, especially when one's senses receive negative feedback. Otherwise, an unexpected misfortune could cause him to lose control of himself. Emotional problems like depression and anxiety result, when strong negative emotions choke up one's intelligence and awareness, forcing one to think negatively. This could be a biological error in many cases. It is also possible that one could develop it. One could also correct it with help by changing attitudes.

Freedom for All

Lincoln and Gandhi

We have been discussing the various environmental and individual limitations and weaknesses, and how to overcome them in order to be free. As long as there is slavery within man, society cannot provide us with freedom. The free man, on the other hand, is able to fight slavery in his environment and in society. All great men, like Lincoln and Gandhi, had to offer their lives on the altar of freedom. Let us look at the various limitations and weaknesses in modern society against which we have to fight.

Social Limitations

Social limitations are the sum total of environmental and individual limitations. Space and time limitations would not affect freedom as much as limitations of natural resources. Shortages of food and oil have become very serious problems in our global society. The technological developments in agriculture and industry cannot keep pace with the population explosion. The population of the earth now exceeds seven billion. It is the overcrowded countries that lack adequate food supplies. Exporting food to needy areas is not easy. Overstraining the world's logistical system, shortage of transportation to remote areas, poor administration, and corruption make it difficult. There are now massive birth control programs, prevention of energy wastes, and newer techniques in the food industry. Moderation of consumption by the well-off is essential to solve the problem. In six months, a citizen in an advanced industrialized nation consumes the energy and raw materials that lasts the citizen of an underdeveloped nation for his whole life.

Although declines in birth rates have achieved zero or negative population growth in many Western societies, Africa, South Asia, and South America are still fighting a losing battle. Religious beliefs and illiteracy make it difficult to introduce proper family planning devices in some countries. In India, for example, the government of Indira Gandhi offered a free transistor for anyone who was willing to undergo a vasectomy. Even this could not attract many people. In spite of the progressive Green Revolution in many countries, with machines, fertilizers, and better seeds, for every extra mouth they begin to feed, ten new ones appear. Industrialized countries have to do more to share their food with the hungry world, on an effective administrative level. Inflation, which is thought to be the result of the increase in the population and human needs, and the increasing expenditure in resources and production, can be overcome only if we reexamine our needs and demands. Out of the many solutions by the experts, there is one that everyone could implement: moderation in our demand for luxury items and higher pay for lower income people.

Based on UK statistics, economist A. W. H. Phillips showed that the higher the employment, the higher the inflation. According to him, putting more people to work would increase inflation. On the other hand, in today's experience, more unemployment means more unemployment benefits, which have to come from somewhere. Of course, we need industries to keep people employed. But what are some of these industries producing? Many of those produce unnecessary gimmicks that waste our natural resources. We could employ more people by expanding the occupations and industries, which would take care of our basic needs. More people could be employed by extending programs like developing new and better sources of food and nutrition, better media for transportation and communication, new sources of energy, better health care, more research on epidemics and terminal diseases, treatment of birth defects, and mental and physical handicaps, better education for children to reduce the crime rate in the future society, and better facilities in correctional centers. We don't have to create jobs for people by producing more guns, more cigarettes and liquor, bigger cars, and better nuclear weapons, which produce costly aftereffects. If we are not concerned about the repercussions, war is a good way to keep people employed! Producing more of anything will not solve our problems. We have to produce more of what people need in order to live in freedom and love.

Let us now consider the cultural differences and national barriers that limit man's freedom. One of the better results of British colonialism is that it made the English language universal, thus making international communication easier. Before the British went to many countries, they were conglomerations of small kingdoms of cultural and linguistic differences. Whether European colonialism was good or bad is debatable, but it helped to achieve cultural conformity in many colonies.

International emigration has increased the cultural and racial interaction on the globe. Mixed marriages have begun to erase the clear distinction between colors and physical features in the newest generation. Just as the combinations of letters of the alphabet can produce words many times their number, cultural differences can act as a basis for the proliferation of creativity. But due to recession and unemployment, Canada, the United States, and many Western and Northern European countries have considerably reduced the number of immigrants allowed into their countries.

Society, the Slave of Slavery

Which should be more appropriate to say: "Society is a slave of the individual," or "The individual is a slave of society"? Probably both statements are right. To begin with, the various forms of slavery found in society, are extensions of the slavery within its individual members. This does not exclude the fact that the ideas and philosophies people live by are not their own, but are those of a minority of individuals who have learned to manipulate the whole society for their advantage. People in general have a weakness for things that appeal to their senses. This principle is proved by the fact that man can be manipulated by the sensationalism of the salesman in any industry.

To the Neanderthal men of the Stone Age, consciousness or conscience and religious sense were the outcome of fear toward natural forces like the sun, moon, thunder, and lightning. Anything that was more powerful and beyond their comprehension was a god for them. Their dependency on these powers created in them a sense of wonder and admiration, which resulted in worshipping them or offering sacrifices to them. This was an expression of the helplessness and limitations of these early men. Fertility in land and women was the blessing of gods, which was repaid by offering the first fruits from their harvests. A natural catastrophe was the result of aggravating a god through the unpleasant behavior of certain individuals. Later, when man manifested gods on totem poles and carved stones, his weaknesses began to show in the modes of worship and in social norms. Men thought gods to be as vengeful as themselves, and they believed epidemics, floods, and earthquakes were acts of a mad god whose anger was provoked by someone in the group. Even human sacrifices were thought to be necessary, to pay the ransom. Moral conduct began to revolve around the law "An eye for an eye and a tooth for a tooth."

As man acquired better understanding of the world around him, his ideas about gods changed too. Deities were personified and were thought to speak through the prophets, who were chosen to lead the tribes. Down through human history, we can notice the evolution and modification of the idea of God, and the sense of morality, for the better. The beginning of moral conscience in man was the result of his fear of God. Prophets of great religions made tremendous changes in moral conscience of society, even though at times their human weaknesses advocated bitterness toward enemies. But the laws they brought forward were always better than the ones that existed previously. People who believed the prophets to be messengers of God and failed to recognize their human condition, tried to live by the letter of the laws, often with an attitude of revenge toward their enemies. Even today, there are people who quote a line or two from the Old Testament to justify their negative aspirations. It was not that the Old Testament prophets were wrong, but in modifying the laws in their own times, their conscience was not developed enough to see the need for turning the left cheek to those who slap you on the right, as Christ told his men to do. Christianity, in essence, could never propagate violence. The holy wars were the results of unholy attitudes in the men who inspired them.

The Bed of Procrustes

Inequality is the natural order of things. In the environmental dimension, material objects, plants, and animals differ quantitatively and qualitatively. In the individual dimension, there are physical, intellectual, and sensory inequalities, even at birth. There are the physically handicapped and the physically well coordinated, the intelligent and the slow learners, the mentally disturbed and the mentally healthy. In the social dimension, there is racial, cultural, and economic inequality. It is possible that scientific technology will one day, through experiments in genetics, invent a "procrustean bed," and people would be born without any handicaps. Procrustes was a Greek mythological giant who stretched or shortened his captives to fit one of his iron beds. Some of our democratic institutions sometimes behave like Procrustes, forgetting the fact that people are unequal in many ways.

However, the term equality often refers to economic equality in our society. Complete economic equality is something that could happen in a global family, where people would share their wealth to the satisfaction of everyone's needs, regardless of the productivity of individual members. Such an ideal socialism could only be found in religious monasteries and convents. For the laymen in a society of obstacle races, equal opportunity would not produce economic equality because of their physical and psychic differences. But we are not concerned about economic equality, as much as we are concerned about economic freedom or economic survival.

If in ancient times economic slavery was the result of physical inferiority, in modern times it is more or less the effect of intellectual inferiority. Cavemen established superiority through physical strength. Neolithic men, with the invention of farming, used physical strength to increase possessions and power. Gradually, intelligence overtook physique. With cunningness and covetousness, anyone could establish economic superiority, and the less fortunate were labeled as laborers. Eventually, the rich became richer and the poor became poorer, and often people became rich or poor by birth.

In democratic societies, the division of the classes—the rich, the middle class, and the poor-based on economic standards—is directly linked to intellectual abilities and physical talents. The slaves of the economic system, the poor or the welfare victims, are usually less capable mentally and physically than the rest of the community. Physically and mentally handicapped people are limited in their activities of course, but not by their own choice. In a society in which man's worth is determined on the basis of his ability to produce, discrimination against people limited in physical and mental activities is a natural outcome. The government is gradually realizing the situation, and handicapped people are beginning to be treated with respect.

As far as economic freedom is concerned, individual limitation is a burden, but individual weaknesses are not necessarily so. A corrupt mind can always invent crooked ways for instant economic success. Some of our inner-city schools are only good enough to train children for economic slavery. Children from middle- and upper-class families usually do well in schools. For one thing, in most cases their parents are well educated. Then they have plenty of toys, learning materials, and reference books at home. In many cases, the mother is able to spend more time to look after and raise the children. They have enough money to go places and see things, thus exposing the children to many learning situations. To top it all, the higher income residential areas have better schools.

Some of our inner-city schools, especially in the slum areas, can provide the child with only a "ghetto education." It is in the ghettos that we need schools with the best facilities, teachers, and training. This would be a great investment in the future of the youngsters, who would otherwise be enslaved economically forever. We cannot expect much from the parents of the ghetto families, who themselves did not get a good opportunity, for proper education. It is a fact that conditions in slum areas can psychologically demolish a child, who might grow up with many negative attitudes, which in turn could turn them into criminals. If only a small portion of the money spent on crime prevention and criminal justice were used for value education and psychological help in ghetto schools, we could secure the future of many a child in the slums, both morally and economically.

Lack of opportunities is a vicious restraint to freedom. Overpopulation and the resultant competitions have made it difficult for many of us to make it economically. Another factor is a shortage of natural resources to fill our stomachs and feed our factories. Economic problems, it seems, cannot be solved by industrialization alone. Overpopulation and shortage of natural resources are getting so out of hand that at times we worry about the survival of the human race.

Economists of our time find it difficult to formulate effective measures to stabilize the world economy. According to Keynesian theory, introduced in the 1930s, employment in any society can be enhanced by increasing demand and output. Accordingly, governments should adjust their taxation and expenditure. Monetarists, headed by the Nobel Prize winner Milton Friedman, would not agree. Their argument is that if the quantity of money circulation increases faster than productivity, the result is higher prices. Therefore, by restricting the amount of money circulation, prices would be forced down, because there would not be sufficient money to pay high prices and wages. However, this economic adjustment might cause more unemployment. Perhaps a more justifiable distribution of wages and profits might help. If the low-income groups, who are in the majority, were paid higher wages, they would in turn do more buying. This would increase productivity and employment.

To achieve this, prices should be forced down. Although the industrialists might not increase their profits from prices, they could make it up from the increased productivity. Also, the money for raising the low wages could be found by putting a freeze on the higher wages, and by using the unemployment funds as more people begin to work. This would help close the gap between economic classes. It is sad that there is great variation in the price of manual and intellectual labor. Physical talents are making unjustifiable wages. Many big football and hockey clubs have raised the ticket prices to cope with the greater demand in pay by the players. To provide inexpensive entertainment to the average man, there has to be a limit on the payments to the players.

We cannot wait to solve the problems of starvation and poverty in the world until new sources of food and fuel are found. Unfortunately, the main bulk of the human population is born into poverty and miserable living conditions, and they're unable to get out of the trap. Financial handouts would only make people lazy. Perhaps an effective way to help them is to increase the funds for teaching positive attitudes and proper skills to take care of themselves. This is a question of conscience. To achieve this, we have to deepen the awareness of the problems of our brothers and sisters, forgetting national boundaries and cultural differences. What the governments are doing to help the developing nations are not enough. There should be increased individual responsibility and sensitivity. If we have the will, there are plenty of ways to help. One could take active participation in many voluntary and charitable organizations involved in social reform. If we are not our brothers' keepers, they do not have any choice other than to live and die in economic slavery.

This kind of concern is something we develop through propaganda. Following the footsteps of the great men and women who believed in the international brotherhood of men, one has to speak out and get involved, increasing this awareness in others as well.

Political Freedom

The evolution of authority and leadership from the tribal chiefs to the presidents or prime ministers of modern governments is the history of struggle for political freedom. In fact, any other form of social freedom involving thought and action is directly related to the form of government. Again, if politics or ruling classes have put the people under one form of slavery or another, it was a manifestation of their greed for power and unquestionable authority.

From tribes and tribal chiefs arose kingdoms and kings. The conquerors enslaved the conquered as a form of punishment. Many of the invasions of the great emperors were unprovoked. It was power that they were after, as with the Aryan invasion in India that resulted in enslaving the natives for manual labor and labeling them as untouchables. The ordinary man under a monarchy was denied creativity. Freedom was monopolized by the rich and the ruling classes, who inherited it often by birth. It was the Renaissance and Industrial Revolution that turned things around. The Renaissance marked the age of adolescence for man, with a sudden growth in attitudes and ego, like that which happens to a teenager from age thirteen to sixteen. As a result, people began to question authority. Their desire for freedom erupted in revolutions that overthrew monarchies and enthroned the ordinary man in authority.

The democratic and totalitarian governments of today proclaim that the working class is free. The communistic and militaristic regimes believe that strict censorship over thoughts and actions is necessary to ensure that the destructive and selfish instincts of man are suppressed. What is good for man is dictated, not determined by the individuals. The decisions from the top often do not ensure the freedom to develop one's creative potential. The imposed discipline often threatens freedom of thought, and as a result, we often hear about defections of citizens from totalitarian states to democratic countries. Totalitarian authority tends to treat society as if it were a traditional, teacher-centered, elementary school where indoctrination and imposed discipline are the principles of operation. The enforced strength and solidarity of such a structure lacks the moral support of the individual members. As soon as the external force of authority diminishes, the structure is bound to explode.

Democracy, on the other hand, tends to see society as having come of age and providing better opportunities for self-determination. The unfortunate fact is that society has not come of age. The strength of democracy is directly proportionate to the responsibility of its constituent members. If everyone is there to grab what he can get, free creativity would become an idealistic slogan to be laughed at. The fact that people are allowed to choose, does not mean that people are always going to choose the good. Corruption can always bypass laws that are intended to protect the interests of all citizens. As a result, in most democratic countries we see people losing self-discipline and responsibility. Terrorism in modern cities makes us think that we gained freedom from the forces of autocracy, only to be enslaved by the forces within us. Man cannot overcome the weaknesses within, without some kind of external pressure.

Individual responsibility could erode in the outflow of human weaknesses, and by the temptations of forbidden apples. Some environmental restrictions and at times rigid laws are necessary to promote creativity. Although the legitimacy of Indira Gandhi's procedures toward greater autonomy over the Indian parliament in 1975 was questionable, it provided the country with greater social and economic security. With a population of over one billion and a multiplicity of political ideologies and linguistic and cultural variations, the nation was in severe strife before the declaration of emergency in 1975. Until then, multiparty administrations were collapsing as soon as they took over state governments, corruption and anarchy were mounting, and industrial production was going downhill due to persistent strikes. Because of the complexity and multiplicity of its problems, a country like India needs a strong centralized government to promote creativity. Indira was able to achieve considerable economic stability, eliminate corruption, and thus enable the working class to find economic and social freedom. The 30 percent inflation recorded in early 1974 was reversed by mid-1975. According to official statistics, in September 1975 the price index was 7.8 percent lower than a year before.

Some of her policies and procedures were questionable, many of them were necessary for the nation's internal security. Her censorship policies have to be seen in this light. License for inspiring destructive activities by the media has to be restricted in order for democracies to be effective, especially in counties where most people are not educated enough to distinguish between facts and fables. In a country like India, where political parties proliferate overnight over insignificant issues, and struggle for leadership, antigovernment propaganda for the purpose of political gain was a common practice.

Since independence, the country did not have enough time after the emotional and intellectual warfare over political ideologies, to think seriously about its future. Selective censorship to establish the internal security of a country over a limited period of time is not always too sour to swallow. But the validity of such censorship procedures had to be evaluated in terms of the degree of confusion and corruption in a democratic society. On the other hand, permanent censorship over the free and creative activities of the citizens as practices in many totalitarian regimes is dehumanizing. In a developing country where the majority of the people are incapable of creative self-determination, certain restrictions are inevitable, just as children have to be disciplined at times to develop proper attitudes. Even in developed nations like the United States, dehumanizing activities have to be censored in order to control organized crime and mishaps.

The liberal attitude toward the accessibility of governmental information to the public by the US government is a clearly democratic policy. This could help to reduce the executive corruption that has handicapped American administrations in the past. With the new openness of government, many corrupt proceedings of the intelligence agencies are also coming to light. In this connection, it is necessary to supplement the first amendment with efficient legislation in order to defend freedom and prevent destructive social behavior. This is an area that needs more investigation.

The major trouble with modern democracy is excessive capitalistic manipulation. Politicians and political parties are supported and sustained by big industrialists, on whose strings of manipulation, senators, and MPs, act like puppets, when making decisions for the common man. This, together with the lack of interest from the lower class during elections, adversely affects the socialistic aspects of democracy. In these respects, social welfare programs for the lower class in most democratic countries, can only be a socialistic overcoat on capitalism. Even free enterprise is being plagued by capitalistic manipulation. To start a business these days, one has to possess fairly high levels of material assets and financial credits.

Crime is a by-product of capitalism. The feasibility of the crime depends not only on the criminal attitudes but also on the environment. If a man has a tendency to lose his temper and become physically aggressive, he might hit someone. If he has access to club, he might use it instead. If he carries a gun, homicides could result. Restrictions are necessary. However, people make the laws. Gun control is opposed by the majority in America. Along with protection against crime, programs for crime prevention in individuals should be incorporated within the educational system, in schools and especially in correctional centers. A series of small break-ins and cover-ups could amount to Watergates of an ill democratic conscience.

Correctional centers often fail to produce the desired results, and in many cases they act as factories where minor criminals are turned into major ones. Locking up and letting out the offenders will not create any magic. Rehabilitation has to be a step-by-step procedure in which the antisocial elements are rooted out, and the person becomes more adaptable to normal life. Correctional centers could include operations and industries where the convict would be given the opportunity to accept responsibility and put his potential to work productively.

The history of the twentieth century has been written in blood as wars and violence steadily tortured the inhabitants of earth. Aside from the big wars, individual incidences of violence have been steadily rising in the international scene. In the United States, the number of murders committed has more than doubled in the past twenty years. The Federal Gun Control Act, passed in 1968 after the assassinations of Robert

Kennedy and Martin Luther King Jr., was never effective. It is estimated that the average sale of handguns in the US are in the millions per year. Juvenile involvement in homicides is increasing at an alarming rate. Independent studies at various institutions reveal that there is a connection between violence and media publicity. The more publicity given to kidnapping, bomb threats, or gun violence, the more incidents there have been. This could be due to the desire for instant attention by some villainous criminals. Mostly the victims have been innocent people. Organized crime also seems to overpower the police force and the judiciary system. Any authority given to the police to assure internal security of a country, rather than to demolish some political opponents, would be a strictly democratic measure.

Spare Rib of Man?

The biblical story of the creation of woman from man's rib conveys the message of unity between man and woman. Long before mechanization, when people lived on manual labor, physical strength had authority. Men were the breadwinners; women cleaned up the house and took care of the children. There was a kind of master-servant relationship between husband and wife. Men who spent most of their time outdoors fighting with the animals had enough muscle power to earn fear and respect from their women. Men took women as they acquired cattle, for their service and comfort. Kings and emperors of many ancient civilizations had plenty of women. In many cases, their relationships with women were not much different from that which they had with wine. To this day, polygamy is prevalent and legal in many parts of the world.

In arranged marriages of the past, many women could not even have a look at their future husbands before the wedding. The first sight would have been an unpleasant surprise in many cases. The parents of the couples made all the arrangements. Women had to pay a dowry to get a husband. The uglier the woman or the wealthier the bridegroom, the higher the dowry was. Family status was an important factor too. As it happened in some cases, fifty-year-old men from rich families wound up marrying fifteen-year-old girls whose parents thought that they had made a good deal. Arranged marriage has lost its old stigma in many parts of the world, where parents and relatives may try to create a seemingly compatible couple, but whether a love relationship or marriage comes out of it, is up to the individuals themselves.

Education was a way for women to gain social status. Strange as it might appear to be, a male-dominated nation like India was able to produce a female prime minister. Indira Gandhi was able to assume political leadership because of the opportunities she had growing up as the daughter of former Prime Minister Jawaharlal Nehru.

Women in North America are getting more and more into politics and the judiciary. There was a time when nursing and teaching were the only major jobs for women. Today's women are ready to undertake social responsibilities that men thought only they could do. We have women as police, senators, doctors, and even priests. A woman president, or even a black pope are not distant possibilities.

Scientific technology has helped the liberation of women

in many ways. Biological regularities like menstruation and pregnancy do not limit the realm of their activities, as they may have in the past. However, women's liberation does not lie in women trying to grow hair on their chests. Even if technology in the future is able to do away with many of our biological limitations, there are still certain activities that women do best, and there are activities that men do best. Liberation for both men and women could be accomplished by developing the potential in each sex, in its own way.

Women should be proud of the fact that only they can give birth to a child or bring up a child with loving care and great patience. Men need not feel bad about it. There are certain things only they can do.

The Untouchables

Racism is as old as the period in history when different tribes came into contact with one another. Racism has its psychological roots in the suspicion and superiority complex inherent in man, which can produce prejudice against members of other families, other nations, and especially other races. From ancient times, there have been conflicts between different races, as was expressed in the caste system in India and the Shinto religion in Japan. Racism culminated in the West during colonialism.

The caste system in India, which was once the only basis for the social and economic hierarchy, has in recent years lost its credibility, except in villages and rural areas. During the time of British colonialism, it was pronounced throughout India. There were four casts: the Brahmins (the priestly class), the Shatrias (the ruling class), the Vyshias (the merchants), and the Sudras (the laborers, or the untouchables). The Brahmins, the highest in the hierarchy, had to wash themselves clean if they happened to have even accidental physical contact with an untouchable. The untouchables were treated as badly as or worse than black people in America during the time of slavery. Communism in India was, more than anything else, a result of racial discrimination. Even today in many villages, the untouchables are forced to call the others "lord" and must never question their demands. Things are changing.

In the West, the theory of the superiority of the Nordic race, proclaimed by people like Adolf Hitler, Stuart Chamberlain, and Madison Grant, claimed that whites were by nature and heredity superior in color, culture, and intelligence to the rest of mankind, and therefore they were justified in dominating and discriminating against inferior groups. In South Africa, the Nationalist Party introduced apartheid in 1948. The Group Areas Act that followed in 1950 separated races, with 13 percent of the country being set aside for the native Africans. Segregation of the government was essential for avoiding racial and cultural conflicts. The whites in South Africa argued for a long time that because their brainpower developed the country with industries and institutions, and giving political power and rights to the natives would mean the degeneration of the economy through lack of know-how on the part of the natives.

But many other colonies fell, just as kingdoms did, and the uneducated natives began to acquire the skills to run the country. South Africa has followed the same script. Although a more federalized democratic system is advisable even in developed countries, because of the fact that man is self-centered and inconsiderate by nature, it is a must in any new nation emerging from colonial regime due to a multiplicity of problems, including illiteracy. However, there is always the danger of losing individual freedom, due to oppressive totalitarianism, which could inflict a permanent handicap on the self-determination of the citizens. But a strong federal government, with a fair amount of censorship, could gradually give more autonomy to the provincial administration as internal security and economic progress are established. Many African and Asian countries would be better off today if they started off with stronger federal governments immediately after their independence.

On the other hand, militaristic regimes like that of Uganda have terrorized the masses and jeopardized individual freedom.

Though racism has been gradually disappearing from developing countries, racial integration is still a problem. In a world that is filling fast with people and boiling over with discontentment, racial integration can perhaps be postponed but never avoided. It took a while before the black people in North America gained whatever social acceptance they enjoy today. Integration is not easy to begin with; friction and conflicts are bound to arise when racial groups interact, but they gradually disappear. Bigotry is, more than anything else, the result of unfamiliarity and lack of understanding. Athletics and entertainment were the ways into white society for African Americans. When they established themselves in these fields, other avenues of activities opened up for them, and the myths about racial inferiority or superiority began to fall apart. But paramount was civil rights movements.

Urbanization, with all of its demoralizing impact, has done a few good things. The inevitable and massive interaction in the industrial world broke down the barriers between races and people. Men who have to struggle for survival and economic freedom are learning more and more to be tolerant toward members of other ethnic groups. There is still a long way to go before man attains complete freedom from bigotry.

Schools are the most comfortable starting points for racial integration, especially primary grades, where little people are not intimidated by the notion of untouchability. For children who grow up in multiracial environments, the question of bigotry and racism will not arise as much, if they are integrated at an early age. This notion has caught on in parts of the United States, where they try to achieve integration using all available means. Before 1974, there had been very little integration in the city of Boston, where 82 percent of black children were in school with a black majority. In June 1974, District Judge W. Arthur Garrity Jr. accused the school committee of intentionally segregating schools at all levels, and he ordered an integration plan that involved busing about 18,200 of the city's 94,000 public school students. This was met with wide opposition, but the situation eventually cooled off.

Once again, social freedom and sense of responsibly can be reestablished in the newer generation, if our classrooms for early childhood education are imbued with moral concepts. The resistance of children from such a background toward the evil influences in society when they grow up would be much greater than those children who do not receive much self-disciplinary motivation. In fact, a healthy sprout withstands a bad environment better than an unhealthy sprout. Unfortunately, the educational system in North America is not doing enough in the field of value education. It is time we realized that a positive attitude in a child is more important than a 'A +' in arithmetic.

United Nations: The Capital of the Future World?

If ever there is going to be just one government for the entire world, the UN has to be its capital. It does not take a global war to achieve unification of all nations. The UN, with its devotion to the fundamental human rights and values, as well as its interest in man all around the world, has the essential qualifications for a peaceful unification of all nations in the world. The organization, which started off with 51 states in 1945, now has many more members.

It is indeed a fabulous idea to have just one world government, which is in the interest of man anywhere in the world regardless of creed, color, age, or sex. In order for the UN to achieve efficiency, certain fundamental restrictions have to be removed. The General Assembly, in which all the member nations participate, should have absolute power over all the other organs, including the Security Council. The permanent membership of a few big powers in the Security Council (and their right to veto major decisions) are dictatorial as far as the less powerful nations are concerned. Instead, all members should be elected by the General Assembly to protect the interest of all the members. Also, the big powers have to take the UN more seriously. Big power diplomacy outside of the UN will eventually create problems if all the big powers choose to compete on this level.

Hopefully as time goes by, we might be able to see a stronger UN, a superpower whose decisions will bring justice and peace to men all around the world. Problems concerning all nations are increasing with technological advances. Territorial wars, international terrorism, food and energy crises, the population explosion, and environmental pollution could be solved effectively through international cooperation in the UN. Through international cooperation, scientific progress and technological developments, could have much more momentum.

As it is today, each scientific discipline has an isolated world of its own. If there is increased communication across all the disciplines of knowledge, the solutions to problems would be multidisciplinary and therefore more fundamental and effective. The UN could be the meeting ground where all great intellectuals of the world, from all disciplines, discuss human problems everywhere and seek lasting solutions.

4

NOTHING BUT THE WHOLE TRUTH

The Truth

Pilate asked Christ, "What is truth?" Christ kept silent. After talking about truth for two to three years, he did not want to define it for anyone whose intention was to ridicule him. Does man know the truth, or will he ever? Probably he would know a fraction of it, after a lot of misconceptions and erroneous proceedings. The truth about truth is that there are three parts to it: the past, the present, the future.

First, the past. In terms of the past, truth is what was. Do we know the truth about what happened to the universe and its inhabitants so far? We have been trying to find out, and we still are. No one can be sure we will ever be able to discover the absolute truth about the past. The bulk of it is beyond our reach.

As for the rest, the human brain and the mechanical extensions of it, are simply not good enough, for an accurate recording.

Then, the present. In terms of the present, truth is what is. Modern mechanisms can somewhat help man to know many facts about things. The more concrete the object of study is, the closer we are the truth. In other words, objective truth is easier to handle than subjective truth. Psychology is yet unable to undermine all the truth there is to the human psyche. In their eagerness, many scientists often jump to conclusions that have dehumanizing consequences. The problem is that our existence cannot be comprehended by disregarding the essence of our existence.

Last, the future. Truth here is what will be. At the beginning of the two World Wars, the future looked bleak. Somehow we came through. But for today, it is hard to not be pessimistic. Many of us are bewildered by anxiety and insecurity. Even though things might get worse before they get better, my belief is that the worst will improve our spirits, and we will start looking for spiritual security, a treasure in heaven, where the moth of greed cannot get in.

In conclusion, truth is what was, what is, and what will be. Every world religion claims to know the absolute truth about the past, the present, and the future. There are Christians who believe that the Old Testament and New Testament are true. Christ's view of the Old Testament was that it was imperfect for his time. It might have been perfect at the time of its writing. We should be more concerned about its essence rather than the print, the messages rather than the stories themselves. In the present chapter, we shall look at some of the fundamentals of Christian faith and analyze them in light of known facts.

Because many fundamental questions (e.g., the creation of the universe, the origin of life, life after death) are beyond the scope of scientific analysis. What we can do is take what the Scriptures have to say about them and speculate on their possibilities with a scientific frame of mind. The classical conflict between science and theology is due to the fact that, though science evolved and grew in complexity, theology refused to move on. When Christ appeared on the religious scene, the people of his time were hooked on the old laws and traditions. The changes that he brought forward were revolutionary, in tune, and ahead of his time. It was his desire that the theology would evolve with time, which he indicated in his statement about the Holy Spirit (John 14:25), whom his Father would send to teach man. In the general sense, anyone who is sincerely searching for absolute truth should be considered to be influenced by the Holy Spirit.

That does not mean that whatever a person in good spirits speculates or formulates is the absolute truth. Instead, it could be a further step towards truth. Due to intellectual limitations and individual weaknesses, no prophet can be absolutely accurate in his predications. A true searcher should be open-minded and should not be afraid of contradicting some of the accepted beliefs. At the same time, he should not be so selfish as to interpret scientific data according to his own interest, closing his eyes to the unexplainable. A rational man can never be an atheist, but he could be an agnostic. If so, it is his responsibility to keep searching without making premature conclusions. Even if he arrives at conclusions, he should be willing to modify them in light of new discoveries and new knowledge. Let us now look at some of the common religious views on the past, present, and the future, in the light of present scientific knowledge.

Trinity in Atom, Man, and God

Among the world religions, Christianity and Hinduism (vaguely) recognize a trinity in God. In Hinduism there are Brahman, Vishnu, and Shiva. In Christianity there are the Father, the Son, and the Holy Spirit. Like in Christianity, the second in these lines has experienced reincarnation, or incarnations. Krishna and Jesus may be said to be similar. Krishna was a cowboy, and Jesus was named the shepherd.

The analogy could be taken into an atom, where there are three particles: protons, neutrons, and electrons. Protons are similar to the Father, neutrons to the Holy Spirit, and electrons to the Son. The Son is more concrete and more present in relationships, similarly to electrons.

The Electron, the Sensorium, and the Son

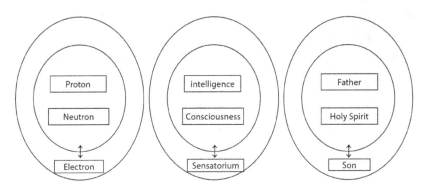

When an atom enters into a relationship with another atom, it is their electrons that do all the negotiations. All the chemical reactions involve the electrons, which exist on the outer shells of the atom. When we heat a substance, the electrons become more restless and move faster. The properties of electrons have a great similarity to the human senses, which are more active than the other two psychic faculties. A human relationship starts with a sensory response, just as electrons make possible atomic and molecular relationships. The deeper the sensory experience, the stronger the affinity, just as electrons become hyperactive with heat. The few opening texts of St. John's gospel lend themselves to a consideration of the universe, as the body of the son (i.e. his material body). After his resurrection, Christ can be thought to be united with the Holy Spirit. Historical Christ, similar to the electrons and the senses, has helped to establish a loving interaction among humans. The Father and the Holy Spirit have remained more or less behind the scenes.

The Proton, the Mind/Intellect, and the Father

The protons have a special relationship to the electrons in the atom. Their opposite electrical charges enable them to have a stable relationship, which contributes to the coherence of the atom. In man, the intelligence and the sense are closely related in a similar way. It is the intelligence that regulates the sensory experiences and perceptions. In the Trinity of God, a special relationship between the Son and the Father is emphasized in the Bible.

The Neutron, the Spirits, and the Holy Spirit

The neutrons in the nucleus of the atom do not take part in chemical reactions, but they can release an enormous amount of energy during radioactivity or nuclear reactions. In the same way, though human consciousness is not as continuously active as senses or intelligence, it has enormous power to do the impossible.

Summary of Trinity in Atom, Man, and God!

I speculate that the neutron makes the protons and electrons active. The spirit or consciousness makes both the body (sensorium, internal and external organs) and the mind (emotions and intellect) active. The Holy Spirit makes the father and the son active.

The Theology of the Origin of Life

If the material world is the Son incarnate, taking on a bodily structure, the corpusculization of the polynucleotides and the origin of the genetic code are beyond scientific speculation. If we look in the Bible for the answer, it says the Spirit of God hovered over the waters during the formation of life (Gen. 1:2). It is possible that the Holy Spirit released or created spiritual units to give life to the complex molecules, and as a result the genetic codes were produced by these spirits, and corspisculization took place.

Human Evolution. Where is it Heading?

There have been many attempts in the past to systematize history as proceeding in a definite pattern. According to one philosophical view, history repeats itself indefinitely for man. However, there are philosophers who think that man, who is getting more and more violent, is going to put an end to human history through wars. The confusion of the twentieth century was grave enough to make many of us pessimistic. If the evolution of the living organisms has had a definite direction with increasing complexity and consciousness, man becoming divine or a spiritual revival is a strong possibility, as Teilhard de Chardin, the French paleontologist, has concluded as a result of his studies on evolution. Based on the theories and speculation that I have outlined so far, it is reasonable to assume that the total human history is comparable to the personal history of an individual, as indicated in the given figure.

The stages in human history can be compared to the different stages in the growth of the human being.

Stage one, represents the life of a child till he is eight. The child's attitude here is one of dependence on his parents and fear toward strangers. This stage is equal to history up to the similar time in BC. Until this time, men feared and respected natural forces, and they depended on them and formed tribal units, just as children under seven or eight form peer groups under a leader.

In stage two (ages eight to thirteen), there is a collective consciousness in the child. He experiences a sense of wonder and has a group approach to problems. This is also a period of great creativity for the child. The period in history from the fifteenth century BC to the tenth century AD, with its civilizations, philosophies, and small scale wars, were similar.

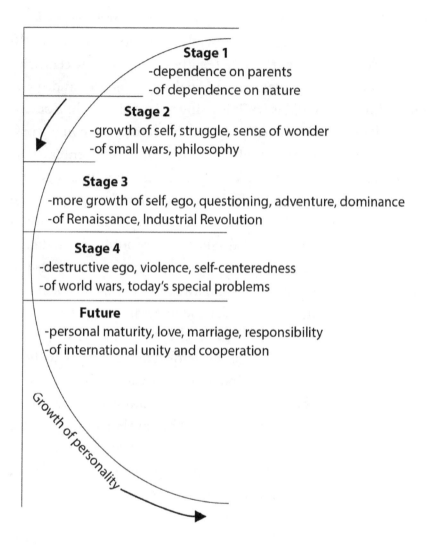

Stage 1
-dependence on parents
-of dependence on nature

Stage 2
-growth of self, struggle, sense of wonder
-of small wars, philosophy

Stage 3
-more growth of self, ego, questioning, adventure, dominance
-of Renaissance, Industrial Revolution

Stage 4
-destructive ego, violence, self-centeredness
-of world wars, today's special problems

Future
-personal maturity, love, marriage, responsibility
-of international unity and cooperation

Growth of personality

During the third stage, from age thirteen to age sixteen, there is eruptive physical and mental growth in the adolescent. This is a period of adventure, questioning, egoistic outlook, and individual concerns. Similarly in history, from the tenth to eighteenth century AD, we have discoveries, explorations, the Industrial Revolution, the Renaissance, and the Reformation.

Then there is stage four. Between sixteen and twenty-four, man is egocentric, aggressive, violent, independent, and self-centered. In history, the nineteenth and twentieth centuries are filled with colonialism, nationalism, violence, and wars, including two world wars. It is going to be quite a while before we pull out of this crucial and most dangerous stage in history.

Generally speaking, after twenty-four, man enters into marriage relationships, takes up responsible jobs in society, and tries to settle down. We have not entered a similar stage in history yet, but there are indications of personal growth, a concern for all humanity, and a sense of responsibility gradually emerging. This is going to happen more and more because of technological developments and awareness of the problems of foreigners, through mass media and intermingling of cultures.

People in each historic age level predominantly displayed the attitudes of similar age levels of man. This has to be a generalization and not an individual case study. If you take a cross-section of humanity today, its mental age is that of an adult aged seventeen or eighteen. That explains many of the problems of society today. But look ahead to the oasis. The future of psychic evolution could be projected in three different areas. Up until today, the emphasis has been on the sensory faculty. In today's world more than ever, people place value on sensory experiences. The main bulk of industrial technology is involved in catering to the needs of human senses. Entertainers in the felids of art and sports are held in high esteem by society.

To get the total picture, you have to compare prehistory to embryonic stages, and history before that to stellar stages!

History is about to enter a new period of intellectual renaissance, along with the sensory faculty. Genetics, electronics, and space sciences are getting ready to inaugurate the era of the intellectual faculty. It is going to be the day of brainpower, and intellectuals will be held in high regard. Prevention of diseases and handicaps, extension of longevity and youthfulness, efficiency in productivity to meet all human needs, and more will become reality. In other words, man will be able to overcome most of his limitations. But his weaknesses or negative attitudes will also be there, creating the possibility of nuclear war.

Even though spirituality will flourish during the era of intelligence, the highest priority will not be given to it until the intellectual era ripens. In the age of consciousness that may follow, many men may develop the powers of their minds and the depth of their consciousness. This may not affect everybody. The good and the evil may flourish side by side. The outcome may be a global war annihilating the inhabitants of the earth. But, just as Christ died and was resurrected, the good may die and be reborn into a heavenly existence, and the bad may be thrown into eternal damnation where there will be "weeping and gnashing of teeth."

The Architecture of the Kingdom

Before the coming of Christ, the meaning of life was not clearly defined. Christ clarified all primitive notions about the reality of life in terms of essence and existence. God created man and gave him the autonomy to experience life through love and creativity. Because of sin or negative attitudes, and especially negative values, creativity is diminished and man cannot find happiness. The only way to restore freedom is through love. And love of man is an offshoot of love of God. But who is Christ? Is he just another man? What is the unique relationship to the Father? These are the questions associated with the mystery of incarnation. According to Christ, he came from above, while the rest of humanity came from here, below (John 8:23). It could mean that man is the product of evolutionary reincarnations, whereas Christ was not. According to Scripture, He was "conceived by the Holy Spirit" (Matt. 1:20).

The Christian Faith

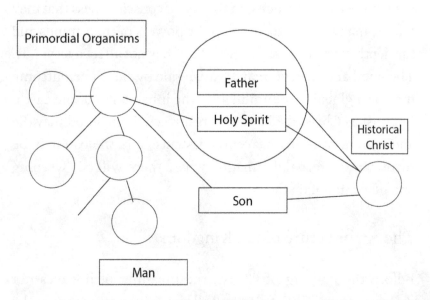

Christ's psyche could be considered to be directly from the Holy Spirit, which has incarnated in the limitations of time and space in a bodily structure. The Spirit, when confined to a physical structure, will take upon itself all the structural limitations. Christ's emotional experiences and intellectual capability in the structure of his brain and body were like those of any other man. The only difference was in the weaknesses. Although other men had very many negative attitudes, Christ did not. This could be due to the fact that he was the Holy Spirit incarnate. Because of this, he might have had access to the ultimate reality and the meaning of existence.

The human psyche could be thought to have come up to the present stage from below, beginning with micro-organisms and working its way up through evolution and transmigration into different physical structures. Man is not that holy anymore. But the Holy Spirit could be considered to be interacting constantly with the human psyche, especially when his consciousness is activated or when he uses the power of self-determination, just as a cancer patient benefits from radiation treatment. The fight against the negative attitudes within man is facilitated through openness to the Holy Spirit. Anyone who struggles to become a better person is actually under the influence of the Holy Spirit, whether or not he knows it. A psychological unity between man and God can be achieved through transcending oneself to the presence of God through prayer. Prayer can either reflect an attitude of helplessness, or an attitude of confidence. In the former, the candidate is like a child begging for a favor, showing an inability to achieve it himself. In a desperate situation, many people call upon God to save them. Prayer with an attitude of confidence reflects a person's faith not only in God but in himself. Christ's prayer to the Father reflected self-confidence and a firm faith in the Father. With such an attitude, he was able to order healings and perform miracles. There are instances of physical and psychological healing, where self-confidence and faith in God work together. Prayer should be supplemented with action. You might have seen weightlifters psyching themselves up before the act. In many cases, it is a matter of affirming faith in oneself without the spiritual dimension. But self-confidence, together with confidence in God, can work miracles. It can help one eradicate offensive attitudes like greed or physical aggressiveness, as well as addictions like alcoholism or drug dependency.

The "spiritual radiation" from the Paraclete might not be visible but anyone who is open-hearted, can receive it in the form of an inspiration or a desire to reach out to others in love. The so-called sacraments can be regarded as proclamations of one's pledge of unselfish love. Unconditional love can be thought to be motivated by the Holy Spirit, even if one is not aware of it. In this respect, baptism or confirmation is a public proclamation of one's intention to love—hence the reception of Paraclete.

In order to prepare oneself to love others or receive the Holy Spirit, one has to come to grips with his negative attitudes or acknowledge that he has such attitudes. In religious terms, it could be admitting oneself as a sinner. A sinner could well be one who has the tendency to take offense often. And one who has such a tendency is often tempted and falls. In this regard, confession should be concerned basically with these attitudes. In the traditional method, in which one gave an account of his offenses against others to a priest, it was presupposed that man was helpless to see himself in the light of righteousness. It was like giving a bath to a child who is unaware of how filthy he is. It was necessary to have a spiritual counselor for anyone not fully aware of his destructive aspirations. People who go to a psychotherapist are in a similar situation. They are helpless to help themselves. Just as adults are capable of washing themselves clean, many people are capable of self- psychoanalysis, and correcting their negative trends. But having a priest or minister to discuss things with would be like having a psychologist as a friend. For many people, this could be beneficial. People with emotional problems definitely need counseling.

According to 1975 estimates, the suicide rates per 100,000 population were twelve in Britain, eighteen in California, and thirty in Hungary. Before a suicide attempt, in most cases there is the death of one's dreams and desires. If living has meaning only, if it offers everything that one hopes for (because society has brainwashed man), a good many people are out of the game for lack of the ingredients, which would make them a material success. Many losers might attempt to commit suicide or try to make it through inhumane means. To a great extent, the breakdown of moral principles and the loss of purpose in life are the results of pedagogy of the so-called scholars who proclaim that life is a gigantic accident. To the laymen, this could mean that life is too short to be wasted, and therefore money should be made quickly no matter whose ribs get broken. Living "how" can have meaning only if living "for what" and "why" are meaningfully answered. Living for oneself would make the answer to living "how" devious. Psychotherapists, who determine the past experiences of a client through psychoanalysis in order to get to the roots of the problem, should realize that a permanent solution to the problem can be found only if life is valued beyond its material merits.

Because humanism disregards the essence of existence, it tends to deny the spiritual evolution of man. It is true that man has innate positive attitudes, just as he has negative ones. But the creative zeal in man has its origin from the creator. Through evolution and incarnations, it is inherited by man. The more man puts God away, the less his chances to grow in love and evolve into a better human. The degree of goodness that man has in him today was cultivated through his religious experiences, down through history. Those who accuse religion of handicapping the growth of human personality have to realize that without religious experiences, however primitive they were in ancient times, the human consciousness or conscience could not have had attained positive standards. Instead, it would have degenerated into a much worse condition. Modern societies with their disregard for God have shown symptoms of the degeneration of human personality. Existence would not have meaning without relationship to its essence. Most of the greatest humanitarians the world has seen were spiritualists. To dedicate oneself to the service of others without expecting a return in money, power, or popularity takes man of God.

One of the fundamental doctrines of Christianity, is the resurrection of Christ. According to scriptural descriptions, after resurrection the spirit will not be limited in material structure, but matter will be at the disposal of the spirit. Even through such a transformation could take place through death, resurrection has to be understood in its totality in terms of evolution, as Teilhard de Chardin conceptualized. The bread and wine of the Last Supper, which Christ referred to as his body and blood, could be extended to the whole material world, which the incarnated spirits use as energy sources. By using material energy either as food or even as sources for creativity, man is gradually resurrecting the universe. Resurrection in the subjective sense is the attainment of spiritual perfection. In the objective sense, it is the creative use of material energy. Christ's body was the same as anyone else's body in that it was made of matter. All the energy that Christ derived, he used for creativity and love. He had to lay down his life, standing firmly for human freedom. This could be the meaning of the consecration of bread and wine by Christ during the Last Supper, and this should be the meaning of the mass. The body of Christ one receives at the altar is symbolic of the fact that the energy one derives, whether it be through potatoes or tomatoes, has to be used for creativity, thereby contributing to the objective and subjective resurrection. In reality, subjective resurrection is the one that counts. Objective resurrection would follow it.

The Evolution of Life, Reincarnation, Heaven, and Hell

We discussed previously the evolution of life on earth, emphasizing the reasons to believe that each species lost its power of further developing its self-determination to the new species it brought forth, carrying on the process of evolution. The species asserted themselves at their own level, incapable of further evolution. As suggested earlier, disease-causing organisms could be considered the "fallen angels", who revolted against their creative assignment by God, and who were thrown into eternal damnation or hell with only an urge for destructivity. With regard to the rest of the organisms, the destructivity developed in them to varying degrees through the influence of the already fallen organisms. In purely spiritual form, these organisms would be many times powerful, because they would not be limited by a molecular structure. Also, as we speculated earlier, the story of the forbidden fruit and the serpent influencing Adam and Eve, suggests that man developed his negative attitudes from the environment. However, he retained his power of further developing his self-determination and therefore the capacity for further evolution into better species, if not a different one. If indeed we accept that life on earth is a one-shot affair and that people should be judged by their actions, how can we accept the fact that a child who dies at the age of two or three is not given the same period of time to prove himself as good or bad, as another person, who is born into a bad hereditary and environmental situation and turns out to be a criminal? How can we explain the miserable living conditions into which some people are born? The theory of evolution also indicates that believing in reincarnation is a rational thing to do. Christ himself indirectly indicated the possibility of reincarnation when he said that John the Baptist was in fact Elijah, the prophet whose return people were expecting (Matt. 11:13). If life on earth were a one-time affair, Christ would not have called back the many departed souls to life again. Instead, he would have told their relatives that the dead had gone to heaven and would have no more interaction with the material world. Jesus advised the sick man he healed to refrain from sin, or something worse would happen to him (John 5:14). This shows a connection between sin and illness, and explains why some people are born into miserable living conditions. This kind of punishment need not be immediate. In some cases, one might not start paying for his criminal activities (sins) until his next life. It could be through a fatal disease, a catastrophe, or a born handicap. A rebirth into a lower species is also a possibility. Great prophets in history probably came back again and again with the mission of bringing people closer to God. When Jesus said that Abraham had seen his days (John 8:56), he might have meant that Abraham had been living in his time. As far as heaven was concerned, Christ said that no one had gone up to heaven except the son of man, who came down from heaven (John 3:13). This could mean that up until Christ's time, no one had escaped the cycle of reincarnations, into a state of being, that is unaffected by environmental, individual, and social limitations and weaknesses, and is unlimited in one's possibility of creative interaction with matter and other souls. This idea was reinforced by Christ when he said that there were many rooms in his father's mansion, and he was going to prepare a place for everyone (John 14:2).

Even through the spirits react with matter during life and after death, the experience of heaven is within a person. This can be explained by an image. When one goes to a concert, the music, the people, the lights, and the whole environment creates an enjoyable experience. But if he went to the same place when there is no entertainment, audience, or lights, the place would not give him the same experience. In the same way, the experience of heaven would be within man, even though matter and a material environment would be involved in experiencing it.

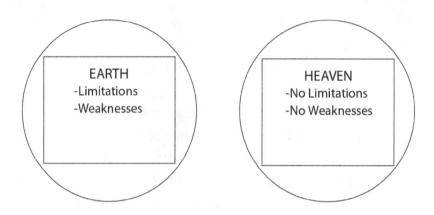

Heaven could be a spiritual state that ensures environmental, individual, and social freedom. In such a state, creativity is unlimited because the psychic potential would be fully developed, and there would be no negative attitudes in any being. Love would be the only law, which is self-induced by each being. Everything positive that you could think of would happen in the absence of disease, death, pollution, handicaps, violence, discrimination, and the struggle for existence. Creativity would be there, and love would be there. Now, this state of heaven need not be confined to a particular planet or a particular space, because the psyche would not be enclosed in a particular material or bodily structure. Instead, the psyche would be able to assume any physical structure whenever it pleases. In other words, man would not be manipulated by his bodily structure as he is on earth. On the other hand, in heaven, matter would be under the complete domination of the soul.

The narratives of people who claim to have had an out-of-body experience and a taste of heaven project heaven as a state of experience of maximum freedom and love. First, sensory experiences are said to have intensified to the point where the person was able to see colors most vividly and hear sounds most melodiously. Also, there is mention of a feeling of lightness, which could mean the complete dominance of matter by spirit. The intellectual faculty is said to have attained complete freedom, in that the person had complete knowledge of all the truth, before returing to the body.

Consciousness also had full freedom, in that there was a radiant love and joy for the spirits. Such a state of heaven, beyond worldly limitations, could be accessible to anyone who attains spiritual perfection. On the individual level, limitations like handicaps and lack of talents would be undefeatable perhaps, but weakness or negative attitudes have to be defeated to attain spiritual perfection. Exploitative attitudes have to be replaced by love of God and man, expressed through action. Until that stage, one could be born again and again into levels of heaven, depending on the degree of spiritual perfection that he attains in each life. Anyone who is aware of his sinful attitudes and constantly struggles to overcome them, will be in the purgatorial state. Spiritual perfection has to be evaluated in terms of the basic attitudes or intentions. Someone who is devoted to serving others, for the sake of love, will have attained spiritual perfection in spite of the fact that self-centeredness once in a while emerges in his activities. Temptations and struggles were part of even Christ's life. The man who attains spiritual perfection would be completely honest to himself and open to others in his affairs.

Heaven is relative to human attitudes and activities. All the human energy is basically channeled toward building a heaven on earth by trying to overcome environmental, individual, and social limitations and weaknesses, thereby being able to enjoy life in freedom and love. Therefore, the kingdom of heaven is here and now, within everyone to varying degrees, although the full realization of it is far away. Keeping one's negative attitudes under control and dealing with people with love are not easy tasks, and so the road to the kingdom of heaven is narrow and filled with hurdles. However, for anyone who tries to give of himself for others, there is great reward in the form of self-satisfaction, and at times appreciation, by others, which is expressed through their love and gratitude. Great humanitarians, who dedicate themselves to others, experience heaven within themselves in spite of the sleepless nights of creativity and manifold obstacles. Facing the challenges of life and putting up with troublesome environments and situations, while reaching out to others in love, are greatly satisfying experiences for a man of God.

The road to hell is wide and easy to ride. It is easy to hang on to passions and hang-ups, to entertain one's own self and turn people off. If reincarnations can successively move one closer to God and humanity, it can also move on away from his fellow beings and God. As a result, reincarnation into a lower form of life, a lower realm of physical and psychic activities and enjoyments, is possible. Many of the creatures in a desert like the Sahara, engaged in a vicious, constant struggle for survival in adverse surroundings, would be in a purgatorial stage close to hell. From there, they can either degenerate into highly destructive disease organisms or progress into a state of more creative existence and better conditions.

As mentioned before, all living organisms can be thought to be at varying levels of heaven or hell. A dolphin, with its positive attitudes, intelligence, and playfulness, is a much higher spiritual existence than a shark with its rebellious, destructive attitude. There are many organismic or botanical existences with greater creativity than many humans. A creative human being who is far from having a firm control over his negative attitudes, might assign himself, through reincarnations, to be a highly creative subhuman organism, for a period of time. The state of such creative organisms could act as a rehabilitative stage on their way up.

If human evolution is successful in building a heaven on earth, eventually all beings will be resistant to diseases, organisms, and evil spirits. But heaven on earth would be the result of a spiritual evolution, more than intellectual or sensory evolution. Spiritual evolution means developing a positive consciousness and increasing creativity. This could be an ongoing process through transmigrations of souls, and death could only be a short stop in between. But the short stop could be longer in some cases, in which an opportunity for the living to communicate with the dead may exist.

The Body of God

Galaxies resemble one another in many ways, like the cells in a living body. Living organisms in this cell of God called the Milky Way may start migrating to other cells someday with the advance of space sciences. It is possible that there is life in other galaxies, other cells of God. The enzymes and organisms in some cells may perform more vital functions than the occupants of other cells. Similarly, in the body of God, some galaxies may contain living beings carrying on more important activities than the inhabitants of other galaxies.

There may be galaxies that promote freedom, love, and truth, or the gradual attainment of these values, without being held down by forces of evil. In such galaxies, there could exist a heavenly environment. A rebirth into such an environment could mean a heavenly existence.

The spirit of God pervades the material universe just like the spirit of man pervades his whole body. The spirit of Anti-God and the evil spirits won over by the Anti-God wait to exert more and more of their influence in the world, to win over more spirits. All the created beings, including man, are vulnerable to the temptations of the evil spirits or demons. The temptations to break the laws of love or commit sin have always been there for man. The influence of the evil spirits are powerful. When one loses his control over himself, or when one is taken over by strong, negative emotions, the result is taking offense or committing sins.

In psychiatry today, most psychotics are brought back to self-control and reality with antipsychotic medications. In many acute psychoses, there is a loss of awareness of the environment, self, and others. In many cases, many repressed feeling that are buried in the subconscious mind may come out. This may cause acting out because many of the subconscious repressed feeling are evil in that they are either the product of a lack of love that psychotics have experienced through life, or the many temptations of social evil that they have resisted for so long. In this respect, many psychotics could be thought to be influenced by social evil. The source of social evil is the evil forces that we talked about earlier. Therefore, even if psychotics are not controlled by evil spirits, often they are controlled by evil in their subconscious psyche, which causes bizarre behaviors. I am not trying to establish a strong connection between psychosis and the influence of the evil forces on the victims, in all cases. There are psychotics who are hung up on strong religious feelings, and there are also organically produced psychoses. Evil spirits have been known to possess humans and to haunt houses. They are like the beasts or animals who run away if faced firmly. For that reason, they do not bother anyone who is not afraid of them, or who does not indulge himself in their fear. Perhaps this is why demonic possessions are predominantly found in people and cultures who fear these spirits or who entertain dreadful thoughts about them. In the case of such psychotic behaviors, in which one loses total control over the self and behaves destructively, it may be that the individual has come under the influence of the evil spirits. This is not to suggest that all the psychotic behaviors are due to demonic possessions. But in psychotic behaviors in which Christ exercised the demons, such demonic possessions were possible. To think that some psychotics are influenced by evil forces is justifiable.

My Ambition
(a leprosy monument)

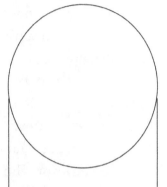

Leprosy is the most
despicable disease
and the most
stigmatized ever!

(Depictions of
people with leprosy
at different stages
of withering)

Monument@EndLoeprosy

FRAGMENTED, REMNANT THOUGHTS

The following topics may be a complete departure from the texts so far. The thoughts hereafter are the result of re-evaluation of previous thoughts, as they evolved. You may demur at some of my inferences. Read on; the ideas are easy to digest!

1) On Design and Assign

The concept is that a concentration of energy beyond thought exploded to create this universe. There may have been such explosions, which does not have any boundaries (i.e., no beginning and no end). The so-called primordial explosions may be happening simultaneously, unlimited times, even as you read this. There is no concept called nothing. Even in outer space, beyond any scientific principles, there is something. Properties of God include space and time without limits. With explosions came sub particles, particles, pre-life, and life, to from micro- to macro-organisms with physical, chemical, biological, and even neurological properties.

Each was designed and assigned to do certain jobs. Scientific principals are converging. Physics, chemistry, biology, psychology, psychiatry, neurology, and even astronomy and astrology are converging into one science: the science of the universe!

2) God is dead?

According to the 2nd law of thermodynamics, "Energy can neither be created nor destroyed!" And, God, who I think, is "Supreme Energy", personified as the Father, the Son and the Holy Spirit in Christianity is the most sensible understanding! ~~The world, is an illusion? Think of 'the very concentrated matter' exploded to create 'this galaxy', starting with sub-atomic particles to objects of all sorts, i.e.. 'The colorful nature, even, airplanes, architecture, shape, colors, texture, species, all came from concentrated matter. If your eyes were microscopic, we only see everything molecular!~~

3) The world is an illusion!

Ultimately, the source of all 'energy' can be traced to God! This Universe began with explosion of extremely concentrated matter (energy) to form sub particles, elements, compounds, objects of different shapes, color, density, metals, non-metals, lights, the nature, and micro to macro-organisms and their organs! All are different forms of the fundamental Supreme Energy, GOD! The Hindu thought that 'the world is an illusion' makes total sense to me!!!

If our eyes were microscopic, we see everything molecular!

4) On God and Anti-God

God by definition is omniscient. He could have foreseen the rebellion of Lucifer and his legions (a Christian belief). If God prevented this rebellion, the world would have been a better place. So, there may be a God and Anti- God. This is just speculation. To believe that God has two sides to his nature (i.e., both good and evil) is unthinkable. But good and evil exist. If there is a dichotomy in God, it may be presented in Hinduism. In the Hindu Trinity, Lord Shiva is the god of destruction! In the universe, in both living and non-living, there are different degrees of good and evil. There are the wild and the tame, the predators and the prey. In man, there is despair and hope, arrogance and humility, grieving and rejoicing, criminal and righteous, giving and taking, angry and compassionate, and more. Even from childhood, there would be mischievous or good-mannered traits. Either you grow further into it, or you grow further out of it.

Moreover, there are bacteria causing leprosy! Bacteria helping bodily functions like digestion. Cancer virus, COVID virus, probiotics and antibiotics and the list goes on. There are creatures who build up and creatures who tear down, on varying degrees. Come to think of it, GOOD AND EVIL have been in never ending conflict! The sum and substance of all evil forces, I call Antigod!

However it is the genes that develop into total being, Christ-like genes will have no sickness or sinfulness and lead to resurrection and eternal life! Devil-like genes will have sickness and sinfulness (Corona itself) and may lead to spiritual death and eternal damnation!

5) On the Living and the Dead

All systems of the body (i.e., integumentary, nervous, cardiovascular, respiratory, digestive, excretory, endocrine, muscular, skeletal) are functional only if a spirit permeates it. A dead may have all those systems, but they may not be working. Spirit gives life!

6) On Spirit, Spiritual, and Religious

Spirit gives life to the living. Religious has to do with doctrines, dogmas, traditions, culture, practices, and the like. I think spirituality has to do with fundamental values like love, freedom, and truth, as well as the positive application of attitudes, values, and habits. One can be religious and spiritual, either, or neither. I believe that spirituality seeds in the genes and sprouts in the brain, when enlightened. Genes may be addictive, obsessive, impulsive, or compulsive. Such genes may fail in bad environments. However, one can have spiritual entity as well as sinful entity. When grown, the dominant personality overrides.

7) On Body, Mind, and Spirit

I think if the trinity in man is segmented into physical, mental, and spiritual, the following could be better understood. There are the physically challenged and the physically sick, the mentally challenged and the mentally ill, and the spiritually challenged (stunned) and the spiritually ill (sin and crime).

8) On Karma and Dharma

Karma, to me, is one's destiny, the way life unfolds. There is the good karma and the bad. Karma may last thirty to one hundred years, or even more. It may have to do with stellar motions and activities. Bad karma could be off set with dharma, or good deeds. When Christ healed the paralytic, he told him, "Sin no more, or worse things will happen to you." Christ also said the trees that bear bad fruits will be cut off and thrown into fire. His proclamation, "There will be weeping and gnashing of teeth," could denote that the evildoers will be born into genes and environments with great suffering. Christ was mostly about works of mercy and love. St. Paul's theology is slightly different, I think. Grace is a gift that need not be earned—it's free. But he said if you do not have love, you are nothing. So maybe grace and works need not contradict. Maybe they are congruent.

Karma or destiny could be predominantly good, bad, in between, mixed, or even intermittent! Sainthood could be accomplished by spiritual evolution through incarnations, or by a life-changing experience!

9) On Common Grounds of Religions

Most religions have a lot in common, especially Hinduism and Catholicism. The Trinity in Christianity is similar to that in Hinduism. In both beliefs, the second person (son and Vishnu) reincarnated. The difference? The Son incarnated as Christ, but Vishnu had many incarnations. Baptism in Christianity is similar to purging in Ganges, to wash away sins. Pooja is similar to mass. Both have the telling of beads. Both believe in nonviolence. I like the Catholic belief of spiritual detoxification. There are examinations of conscience and acknowledgement of one's sins, confession, repentance, and absolution.

10) On Pro-life

The sperm of man or egg of a woman is permeated by their spirits. If left outside, it loses its spiritual energy and dies. But when united in the right milieu, a unique spirit gives it life. Test-tube babies, or even cloning, is possible. A spirit has to permeate!

11) On Immaculate Conception

I believe Christ was born without sinful genes, without blemish. He was born without original sin. To get the highest grade genes, Mary's ancestors had been genetically purified through generations, until genes without evil tendencies were created and Jesus was born without sin.

12) On Energy Crisis

The ultimate future of energy is solar (stellar). We have been exploiting the earth inside and even outside. There needs to be an accelerated attempt to go solar. Hot countries, airplanes, houses, cars, could be retrofitted to go solar. There has to be a will, a strong one. Environmentally, it is a must!

"Global Warming"? There needs to have an emergency meeting with all the UN members right away! No more icebergs melting? Fire, floods and such, all over! People are dying every second! In the 70's, there were talks about 'solar energy platforms' for constant solar! Solar panels are here and that is not enough! Look up! Unlimited stellar! Do something?

Nuclear fusion is the beginning!

13) On Dreams and Ambitions

Dreams could change with time and situations. An ambition is a must-have! To realize, you need a plan. Break it down into steps. First steps are difficult. When you get to the midpoint, you will find that you have a lot of lifelines, the lessons you learned while getting to the midpoint. Then your ambition becomes tangible. Self-indoctrination is important. Tell yourself time and time again what you want to accomplish. Say it aloud, or write it down. You will realize your ambition!

When you write down what you want to accomplish, physically, mentally and spiritually, self-improvement is possible. Read it over often and be preoccupied with them. Break it down into steps. Point A to M may be difficult. When you reach M, the rest of the way to Z is easier, because you have a lot of life lines like experiences and wisdom. Always remind yourself who you are and what you want to become!

14) The Creation and Evolution

Crevolution

Creation is a dynamic process without a beginning. It is ongoing and without end. Both evolution and creation need not contradict, but they coincide. The seven-day creation was written for simple minds. Days could be eons. The sun and earth are needed to call a day, a day. Children are told the sun rises in the east and sets in the west. They don't understand cosmic functions. If you tell them that much, they can grasp it.

First, let me tell you that the Spirit of God that hovered over water (liquid soup) is the Holy Spirit that created the life forms. In terms of behavior of the unicellular to multi, the differences are in the structure that limits or expand the sphere of activities. Spirits may have reincarnated in different structures from simplest to complex. Man is different. He is like the space ship that broke the boundaries of gravitational pull. While other creatures adapted or adjusted to the habitats, man changed the habitats. Consider man from cave to bionic! It is said that God breathed Holy Spirit into man. So, man is in the image of God with unlimited, infinite possibilities. This was possible by the complexity of the structure of the human brain that evolved. Holy Spirit can lose its luster because of genetic defects, environmental defects and limitations and need to be rejuvenated.

15) The Lamb and the Lion

Genetic modification technology, may one day be able to modify a lion's behavior, so much so that the lion and the lamb could live in harmony.

16) All men are created equal?

In man, there are physically challenged and the physically ill, the mentally challenged and the mentally ill and the spiritually challenged (stunned) and the spiritually ill (sin and crime)!!!

17) A word about the spirit

As I mentioned before, it is the spirit that makes all internal and external organs work. With reincarnations, the spirit may gain or lose its luster. In man the brain structure (esp. cortex) is developed to the point his spirit (Holy Spirit) can inflame the total human! Like a spaceship getting out of earth's gravitational pull, man may one day, evolve into a supernatural organism.

18) The Meaning of Salvation

Before Christ, history was destined to die off. With the cross and resurrection, history was resuscitated. I believe that, redemption for mankind was accomplished through, Christ's teachings, his works, crucifixion and resurrection, all of them, summed up together!!!

There are hundreds, may be thousands of religions, in as many countries, and as many gods, stardom, power and even glory! The final destination is Jesus Christ! In order to get there, you may have to be reincarnated, may take unlimited or limited times. In those re-births you may get an opportunity to find Jesus or may not. When you find Him, you are blessed! Then, and then only, you get saved, I believe!!!

Just the beginning……………..

CPSIA information can be obtained
at www.ICGtesting.com
Printed in the USA
BVHW092049050422
633050BV00001B/51